TRAVEL ANYWHERE

(and avoid being a tourist)

FATH★M

Travel trends and destination inspiration
for the modern adventurer

TRAVEL
ANYWHERE

(and avoid
being a tourist)

Jeralyn Gerba and Pavia Rosati
Founders of

www.fathomaway.com

PART I

Starting Out

The World Is Waiting

We are in the midst of a golden age of travel.

One that's more democratic, open-minded, and convenient than last century's, aided in no small part by our interconnectedness, new products, and technologies – like Google Maps, Airbnb, and Instagram – that have forever changed how we explore the world. The evolution of the tools that help us travel has not only shaped the way that we travel, but how and when and where we go.

This is true for both the traveler and the tourist, who may visit the same places but see them in different lights. The differences have less to do with where they are than how they interact with their surroundings. (After all, some people live as tourists in their own town.)

The tourist travels for pleasure, content to skim the surface, stay on the property, eat what they recognize. It's so easy these days. Planes connect to more places. Ships navigate more waters. The most casual of tourists can cruise to Antarctica, roam the plains of the Serengeti, and city-hop with relative ease. With access and spontaneous decision-making, people can find themselves in new places without doing much prep or learning anything about cultural context or local etiquette. With a few quick transactions (flight, Uber ride) and a selfie in front of the most popular spot, the tourist's work here is done.

Like the tourist, the traveler also sees the world as an opportunity for infinite pleasures. But the difference is that the traveler is compelled to seek out the joy – along with fear, frustration, and humility – as authentically and actively as possible. The traveler is determined to get a glimpse of life as a local in a foreign place.

The traveler sees the act of traveling as a proxy for change, for self-discovery, a means of measuring oneself in the world. They know innately or have learned firsthand that some of life's biggest challenges, heartbreaks, and stagnations are remedied by an epic trip. That a cure for loneliness is a dose of fortifying solitude or of unexpected connection. That great romances can begin with a change in altitude. With the right mindset, a three-day weekend close to home can shift a traveler's perspective, mood, and state of being. What a difference a day can make.

BIRDS OF A FEATHER

We have excellent news for you. There's never been a better time to be a traveler in the world. The traveler wants to:

· make new friends at an underground dinner club in Copenhagen
· learn to surf the Pacific in Nicaragua
· spend a month teaching math and English to kids in a small village
· bathe their way through remote ryokans in Japan
· sleep in a tent under a star-filled sky in Montana.

So how, when, and where? These are the questions at hand for us at Fathom (come find us at fathomaway.com), our travel website and agency, where we have spent nearly a decade gathering a treasure trove of timely and time-tested recommendations and stories from a network of interesting people who travel well (chefs, novelists, designers, innkeepers, musicians) in places both well-known and off the beaten path.

As reporters and editors, we have always reveled in the thrill of discovery and the ability to share our most exciting finds with like-minded readers. As travelers, we appreciate the opportunity to try out different versions of ourselves – adventurers and beach bums, gluttons and history nerds, hobbyists and obsessives, volunteers and voyeurs, aesthetes and athletes, ambassadors and enthusiasts.

Along with compelling anecdotes, tips, and gorgeous imagery, in this book we try to deliver a thoughtful and clever approach to being a better traveler and global citizen – covering everything from how to go off-grid, to where to go for a once-in-a-lifetime meal, to cool ways to give back and do good along the way. Our suggestions, while organized by theme, are presented in no particular order – these unique experiences can't be ranked.

Our aim is to help you navigate through the full traveler's journey – celebrating inspiration, experience, and transformation.

Whether you live to travel, travel to live, or some combination of the two, this book is about making the world feel a little more intimate and accessible – and no less wondrous.

OUR OWN JOURNEY

If every great adventure starts with the glimmer of an idea, our journey together began more than a decade ago when, as friends and editors at a beloved media company, we started scheming about what our ultimate travel website would look like. First and foremost, it would bridge the gap between old-world journalism, new-world technology, and timeless curiosity. It wouldn't overwhelm us with options but rather would curate places, people, and things that felt like discoveries. Which is to say we wanted to be spared the headache of trawling 100 websites to find the 10 things we needed to know. And we figured that if we wanted it, other travelers would, too.

The seed was planted. Fathom was born. The name we chose reflected our commitment to being both practical ('fathom' is an actual unit of measure) and inspirational ('to fathom' implies deep understanding).

Along the way, we've attracted a community of like-minded travelers who have helped us make Fathom what it is today: a collection of voices and stories that harmonize around a few key ideas of what travel means and why it's so important to keep moving, exploring, and expanding your horizons – physically, intellectually, emotionally, and spiritually.

FUN FACT: The verb 'fathom' originally meant 'to measure by encircling with the arms' and was synonymous with 'embrace.' It is now often used to refer to the act of comprehension, or getting to the bottom of something.

Opposite page, top: L.A. Jackson rooftop bar in Nashville; opposite page, middle: leaning into the Himalayan breeze; opposite page, bottom: Piss Alley in Tokyo; this page, top: starting them young in the Grand Canyon

PART II

Spin the Globe

The Places Everyone Will Be Talking About

Before we go any further, let's make one thing clear: we don't play favorites when it comes to travel destinations. We want to go everywhere. But making a list of the top timely destinations helps us determine where to go now. Places, like trends or people, can have their moments, fueled by forces that are obvious – big cultural openings, national anniversaries, global sporting events – or intangible. (Ever notice how all the trendsetters seem to suddenly flock to a certain island in the same season, as if by magnetic force?)

Why will we soon be hearing a lot more about Matera, an atmospheric city of caves in southern Italy, and Plovdiv, an ancient Balkan city settled on seven hills in south-central Bulgaria? They've been deemed European Capitals of Culture, a designation that spotlights their cultural developments and fuels initiatives and events that will draw an international audience. Lille, France, awarded the World Design Capital designation for 2020, will show off feats of urban planning and develop collaborative design-driven projects in civic spaces.

Elsewhere, and without as much fancy recognition, destinations are making compelling attractions that will inevitably draw more visitors. The recently completed Jordan Trail is a 400-mile (644-kilometer) path across the entire country, from the Fertile Crescent to the Red Sea. It takes about 40 days to traverse the entire route (a fitting number for this biblical land), passing the ancient King's Highway and crossing iconic attractions like Petra, as well as sandstone mountains, desert valleys, and verdant biospheres.

As we set our travel agenda now, we find ourselves especially drawn to destinations that feel like sanctuaries and that inspire goodwill. If you travel to recharge the senses and want to return home energized and engaged, these places will do all that – and more.

Opposite page: Colorful camels at the Great Pyramids of Giza; this page, top: a city day in Ljubljana, Slovenia; this page, bottom: rustic Azores, Portugal; overleaf page: navigating the icebergs in Jokulsarlon, Iceland

ARCTIC

According to a report by the National Oceanic and Atmospheric Administration (NOAA), 'long-term losses in the extent and thickness of the sea ice cover' are the new normal in the ever-warming Arctic. This will take an inevitable toll on the environment and wildlife, which means we need to see it while we still can – and to do so responsibly, with travel companies that are careful about their impact. For travelers, the rewards will be great when sights include the northern lights and the midnight sun, icebergs and glaciers, and majestic wildlife like polar bears, whales, and sea lions. The North Pole (the location of which is always shifting) is shared by Alaska, Greenland, Norway, Russia, and Canada, but Nunavut, Canada's northernmost territory, is the closest land mass. Options for staying there include the Arctic Haven Wilderness Lodge, a 12-room inn on Ennadai Lake powered almost entirely by green energy and run by a family of pioneering Arctic explorers (weberarctic.com). Arctic Kingdom offers an excellent lineup of small group safaris year-round, with activities like hot air ballooning and scuba diving and accommodations in lodges and tents (arctickingdom.com). If you'd rather travel by sea, Ponant's Expedition luxury cruises explore Norway, Greenland, Sweden, and Canada (ponant.com). By rail, Golden Eagle Luxury Trains' Arctic Explorer charts a New Year's tour of the northern lights on the path from Moscow to St. Petersburg (goldeneagleluxurytrains.com).

AZORES, PORTUGAL

Portugal has been flooding our Instagram feeds, and the next place to follow will be the Azores, an autonomous archipelago in the middle of the Atlantic. The chain of nine islands connected by ferries is an off-the-grid dream of land and sea adventures at every level of activity – from whale-watching to paragliding – and altitude – from scuba diving to mountain climbing. It's little wonder that four of the islands (Corvo, Graciosa, Flores, and, most recently, São Jorge) have been designated UNESCO biospheres. The Azores have year-round appeal, but mark the calendar for the Tremor Music Festival in April on São Miguel, June's Sanjoaninas cultural festival, which dates back to the 16th century, and the massive fireworks show on New Year's Eve. Getting here is fast from the U.S. (four hours from Boston, five from New York) and increasingly easy, with direct flights from the east and west coasts of the U.S., as well as several European gateways.

BAJA PENINSULA, MEXICO

The Baja California peninsula in north-west Mexico – long the home of bad Cabo spring break clichés – has become unexpectedly cool, thanks in no small part to a handful of high-design boutique hotels, both big and small, and charming, farm-driven restaurants. At the same time, northern Baja's Valle de Guadalupe has emerged as the new It wine region in the Americas, with wineries and restaurants ready to serve the savvy gastronomes who find their way here. At the southern tip of the peninsula, sleepy Todos Santos is a haven for travelers, surfers, artists, and bohemians, who can now take a new tolled highway from the airport, trading Cabo's traffic and stop lights for a winding road along the foothills of the austere Sierra de la Laguna mountains and through a desert dotted with massive saguaro cacti.

CAIRO, EGYPT

After the Arab Spring and the ousting of two presidents, the political situation stabilized, transforming Cairo into one of the world's fastest growing cities. While the world and the media struggle to catch up, you can still get alone time with the pharaohs. Just not for long. The new Grand Egyptian Museum – the largest archaeological museum in the world – is a billion-dollar undertaking poised to collect the country's most precious ancient artifacts, many of which were looted and scattered in museums around the world and have now been returned to their original home (gem.gov.eg). In anticipation of tourist numbers set to rival those of Paris, Nile river boats and hotels are getting refreshed, refurbished, or rebuilt from the ground up. Fueled by picture-snapping food obsessives, Cairo's homegrown eateries are doing modern takes on traditional Egyptian food, doubling down on the cadre of locavore travelers.

Opposite page: Mexican flags wave overhead in San José del Cabo; this page, top left: the pool at Las Ventanas, Los Cabos; this page, top right: unfettered Azores; this page, bottom: en route to the Giza Necropolis in Egypt

FUN FACT: Talk about a mega checklist: There are 195 countries on Earth today, 34 of which have joined the roster since 1990.

CAPE TOWN, SOUTH AFRICA

South Africa's second most populous city is usually one stop on a packed itinerary that includes the country's famous safari parks, winelands, and garden route, but reconsider your journey: Cape Town is a destination in its own right, a thriving town on par with Buenos Aires and Seoul. The rapidly evolving Victoria & Albert Waterfront district is home to the new Zeitz Museum of Contemporary Art Africa (MOCAA), the first and only museum of its kind on the continent, where Thomas Heatherwick, the architect behind headline-grabbing structures around the globe, adapted an old, abandoned grain silo (once the tallest building in sub-Saharan Africa) into a striking and unpredictable series of 80 galleries celebrating African art (zeitzmocaa.museum). Excellent shopping, food, design, weather, and access to wine country – not to mention favorable exchange rates – make a compelling case for visiting this capital city soon.

CUBA

As Cuba transitions away from 60 years of rule by the Castros, the country has been adapting to an influx of travelers inspired to explore the country as a whole and go beyond daiquiri-fueled Havana nights. Which isn't to say that we don't have great memories of the capital city's well-documented charms, from rooftop restaurants to brightly colored vintage Chevrolet taxis. The next level of travel around Cuba would include Santiago de Cuba, Cienfuegos, and magical Trinidad – all places that most visitors don't typically see. To get truly off the beaten path, the stops would include Camagüey, the lovely colonial town in central Cuba, and isolated and dreamy Baracoa. Rustic island farm stays, bike-packing treks through the countryside, and kayaking adventures in Ciénaga de Zapata National Park (one of the largest intact wetlands in the Caribbean) offer new perspectives on an iconic place. This, you'll hear yourself tell your friends when you return home, is the real Cuba.

FAROE ISLANDS, DENMARK

If it's wild, unspoiled nature you're after, look no further than this remote, self-governing archipelago comprised of 18 volcanic islands located between Iceland and Norway. The rocky cliffs, postcard-worthy red cabins, and rugged natural beauty can be reached with a short flight from a number of countries, including Denmark, England, Iceland, and Norway. But you have to work a little harder to get where you're going than you would in, say, Iceland. You might have to hike for hours at a time to reach your destination. And even then, many islands will remain hard to access. Since opening in 2011, Koks, the islands' first Michelin-star restaurant, has been drawing curious food lovers from all over Europe (koks.fo). The place to stay is Havgrím Seaside Hotel, a 14-room boutique hotel overlooking the island of Nólsoy (hotelhavgrim.fo).

Opposite page: Gazing into the deep blue and green in the Faroe Islands; this page: Dylan Lewis sculpture studio in Stellenbosch, South Africa

This page, top left: Rooms Hotel in Tbilisi, Georgia; this page, top right: Slap Savica waterfall in Triglav National Park, Slovenia; this page, bottom: prized Lipizzaner equestrian horses in Slovenia

GEORGIA

The Republic of Georgia and its thriving capital are on a hot streak. The Eurasian country and former Soviet republic sees almost as many international visitors as its own population, thanks to new flight routes from various cities in Europe and interest from trendsetting travelers flying through Moscow, Istanbul, and Munich. There are so many reasons to visit. The impeccable dining scene showcases distinct east-meets-west cuisine and impressive local wines. Fun fact: Georgia lays claim to being the birthplace of wine 8000 years ago, and NASA studies verify this. Those are some well-aged casks. ('Qvevri' is their term for the giant, underground clay amphora that store wine.) The country is blazing into the future with a collection of boutique hotels spearheaded by Adjara Group Hospitality: Rooms Hotels (with outposts in Tbilisi and Kazbegi), and Stamba Hotel are artsy, innovative, and cool (roomshotels.com). Add to that enigmatic fashion, forward-looking design, a serious nightclub and dance music scene, super-friendly locals, and access to the wild alpine beauty of the Caucasus Mountains, and you have a recipe for travel magic.

SLOVENIA

This small Central European country has been hiding in plain sight since gaining its independence from Yugoslavia in the '90s. What took so long? It's the only nation on the continent that can claim four major geographic regions: the Alps, the Mediterranean Sea, the Pannonian Plains, and the Karst limestone plateau. This rich natural bounty means seasoned skiers, climbers, and outdoor adventurers have plenty to sink their teeth into everywhere. Kolpa Resort, a hip glampsite in the south, is a lovely place to stay during cherry season (kolpa-resort.si). Chef Ana Roš has spent nearly two decades revolutionizing the food of her country, and it's paying off: her restaurant, Hiša Franko, nestled in the Slovenian countryside, has a Michelin star (hisafranko.com). At the same time, the cool capital of Ljubljana, with its burgeoning art, dining, nightlife, and LGBTQ scenes, makes Slovenia particularly relevant to those with their finger on the pulse.

LIFE-CHANGING TIP #01

Check Your Expectations

& enjoy the adventure

Emerging destinations don't always have the same tourist-friendly infrastructure of well-established places. And that's good! You want to be in a place that isn't used to servicing the needs of demanding strangers. It's a good rule of thumb to keep your usual expectations in check and remember that a big reason why you're here is to experience a place that feels truly different. Travel is about adventures both big and small, and that also means taking a detour from your routines and habits. Don't be alarmed if you don't encounter:

English-language signage.
Before you leave, learn a few key words in the language of where you'll be traveling: please and thank you, open and closed, bathroom, etc.

Seamless wifi.
You're on vacation. Get off your phone!

Perfectly reliable ATMs.
You remember how to exchange currency in a bank, right? If not, get ready to learn again. If possible, change money before you leave home and carry enough cash to last until a bank opens.

Late hours of operation.
Not everyone thinks it's important to go shopping at 10pm or on Sundays.

Global chains (Marriott, Starbucks, McDonald's).
Shop local. Rediscover the joys of small mom-and-pops.

24-hour room service.
Or club sandwiches. Or a hotel gym with your preferred fitness machines. Or a business center with a printer. You get the picture. Go for a run along the beach and reconnect with pens and notebooks.

Dietary restrictions (paleo, gluten-free, keto).
Sorry, your trendy lifestyle may not have hit this remote island yet. But their whole, unprocessed local food might be a revelation if you give it a chance. That said, if you do suffer from an allergy, write down specifics in the local language to avoid confusion at restaurants. Your hotel staff can help with this.

Timeless Destinations

The flip side of trendy is timeless. This is true in so many things – in fashion, in food, and, yes, in travel. For every hot new locale there is a trusty and reliable standby, and we mean 'standby' in the best possible way. After all, what's not to love about something that always delivers, rarely disappoints, and usually leaves you feeling great? These things are timeless for a reason, after all.

That's the good news. Now the bad news: you won't be the only one there. We're talking about places that can get crowded. You might find them packed with tourists, sometimes by the busload, and brimming with low-quality trinkets and bad food that scammers try to pass off as local. You might be able to get around this by visiting Greek islands in October instead of August, by seeing the Trevi at midnight instead of at noon, and by booking a hotel in Tribeca instead of Times Square. But on some level you'll just have to grin and bear it and take the bad with the good. Because these places are very, very good, and to skip them because they've been done to death means depriving yourself and your passport of excellent sights and memories.

Opposite page: Picturesque Greece; this page, top: classically Roman setting; this page, bottom: ancient islands never go out of style

THE MEDITERRANEAN
Greek Islands, Amalfi Coast and Capri, the Balearic Islands, and the Cote d'Azur

Impossible glamour. Bottomless bottles of local wine. Languid and effortless lunches. Bright orange sunsets. Clear azure seas. Cliffside retreats. Cool and shadowy grottoes.

Humans had been sailing the Mediterranean for pleasure centuries before the jet set made it their official playground in the 1960s. Ibiza, St. Tropez, Capri, Mykonos: the mere mention of these places evokes scenes of drinking, carousing, eating, canoodling, sunbathing, swimming, and all the other activities that make warm days and cool nights memorable. What is it about these places that keep them forever in the spotlight? Well, re-read the beginning of this entry. There's a reason travelers who make their way here keep making their way back for more, again and again, often to the same coves, restaurants, marinas, and hotels. When you're practically designed for fun, you want to try to hold on to that quality, and these seaside destinations do everything right, ensuring the joy continues from generation to generation.

FUN FACT: Play the part of a midcentury jetsetter with style inspiration from Brigitte Bardot, Grace Kelly, Sammy Davis Jr., Gianni Agnelli, and Alain Delon.

Opposite page: Recommone Bay on the Amalfi Coast; this page, top: sunwashed colors from buildings to sky; this page, bottom: scene from the Acropolis in Athens

A dazzle of zebras grazing in Tanzania's Ngorongoro Crater

CLASSIC EUROPE
London, Paris, Rome

The great cities of Europe have been, for better and for worse, the hotbeds of Western civilization for millennia, the seats of art and literature, culture and religion, politics and society, craft and cuisine. And they're still at it today. They were central stops on the traditional European Grand Tour, the 17th-century precursor to backpacking around Europe with a Eurail pass today. And while these cities – and the people they attract from near and far – excel at many things, the one quality that has kept them relevant is their capacity for reinvention. Rome has the Colosseum and the MAXXI Museum of Modern Art (maxxi.art). Paris has the Palais Garnier and the Opéra Bastille. London has London Bridge (built in the 13th century) and Millennium Bridge (built in the 21st century). They are living, thriving, and ever evolving, and as such are inexhaustible. Can you imagine ever seeing absolutely everything in Paris? Impossible. And that's why we keep going back.

AFRICAN SAFARI
Botswana, Kenya, Zambia, South Africa

The air is still and your heart is pounding so loud in your chest you're sure the five people around you can hear it. You woke up before dawn to make your way to this clearing, tracking paw prints in the grass, passing a patch of just-dried blood. Suddenly, you spy her – just a few feet away, gnawing on an unidentifiable carcass. Nothing stands between you and that lazy lioness. You realize you're holding your breath. Not that she cares or even notices you. You feel tiny in the vast scheme of things – and that's because you are. You came on safari not to collect sightings of the Big Five or of the wildebeest stampede (the stink lingering in your nostrils), but for this: the reminder that Mother Nature lives entirely by her own rules. And you find that unexpectedly soothing and awe-inspiring. Learning about the mating rituals of kudu, the digestive tracts of elephants, the circulatory system of giraffes, the significance of every zebra stripe, termite mound, poisonous berry, and vulture call – and experiencing it in real time – is grounding and humbling. There's no better way to get perspective than to immerse yourself in the wild.

Opposite page: Tokyo skyline; this page, top: Trevi Fountain, Rome; this page, middle: Eiffel Tower, Paris; this page, bottom: African safari sights; overleaf page: Pacific island paradise

THE GLOBAL METROPOLIS
Manhattan and Tokyo

Whatever you do, don't slow down. You've come to the wrong place if you want travel at a leisurely pace, because New York and Tokyo are vortexes of urban energy, throbbing at and thriving on a rapid clip. The people walk faster, talk faster, and demand you do the same. The street styles the kids are wearing change before their suburban peers have had a chance to notice them. Ambitious strivers have flocked to New York City for centuries – to escape, to get out of their small-town life, to seek their fortune and fame, and, probably most significantly, to find like-minded spirits. The visitors who come for shorter stints crave a small dose of the same: the Gotham myth they know from movies, stories, and songs. Across the globe, Tokyo impresses travelers with its efficiency and hospitality. This is a city that knows how to do everything better, from crossing the street and gift-wrapping fruit to commuting to work and using a toilet. Ubiquitous vending machines dispense ramen soup, fresh bananas, surgical masks, and underwear; cafes let you partake in centuries-old tea-making rituals or cuddle with kittens. Of course, both cities also have their quieter sides, their residential neighborhoods and relaxing parks. But these are places that are fundamentally defined by the adrenaline they display and inspire.

PACIFIC ISLANDS
Bora Bora, Tahiti, Fiji

In 1891, Gauguin fled Paris for Tahiti, seeking refuge from the time-bound trappings of Europe and its fussy ways. The sensual paintings that resulted evoke the peaceful, vibrant beauty he found: you can almost smell the flowers depicted in his saturated canvases. He's not the only one who has fled to these specks of land in the remote Pacific Ocean in search of the kind of escape you find at the edge of the world. There are thousands of these islands, perfectly luxurious even when they're absolutely rustic. It's here that Mother Nature flaunts her best work. Picture this: pristine sand, bright coral, crystalline lagoons, and an impromptu waterside picnic made from scallops on the half shell and a squeeze of citrus, served on palm leaves. Is that gentle plink of ukulele coming from the captain? Indeed it is. It doesn't matter if he's serenading the other honeymooners. While we're lost here at sea, gently rocking in the breeze, we all have stars in our eyes.

LIFE-CHANGING TIP #02

Trips of a Lifetime

Don't think of it as a bucket list but rather a checklist of unforgettable destinations – the B-side, once you've played the greatest hits.

ANTARCTICA

An icy wonderland of penguins and polar bears.
Added thrill: approach the architecture of icebergs by ship.

THE FJORDS OF NORWAY

Where mountains meet sea in dramatic style.
Rare chill: absorb the ancient Viking vibes.

MACHU PICCHU

The once-hidden village built by the clever Incas.
On the hill: behold one of the new Seven Wonders of the World.

VENICE

Still floating, still beautiful.
The drill: you're supposed to feel lost.

RAJASTHAN

The colorful land of Indian royalty.
Fabric mill: bring home textiles as souvenirs.

THE SILK ROAD

Retrace the steps of ancient traders.
Historic shill: goods, ideas, and religion moved from Indonesia to China to Persia to Egypt to Italy on this route.

THE SWISS ALPS

For dramatic peaks and ski breaks within an hour of major cities.
Stand still: the hills are alive. The lakes are to die for.

BHUTAN

The kingdom of happiness and Himalayas.
Goodwill: the global capital is the only one that doesn't need a traffic light.

THE UNITED STATES WEST

Where the myth of the American cowboy lives.
Find a grill: dinner calls for a nice, juicy steak.

TUSCANY

The perfect cliché of Italian country living.
Time to swill: Chianti. Bolgheri. Brunello. Vin Santo. Super Tuscan.

THE GREAT WALL

An architectural marvel to this day.
Fits the bill: but it can't actually be seen from the moon.

MOUNT KILIMANJARO

The imposing peak that can actually be conquered.
Get your fill: follow the climb with a trip to the beach.

THE GREAT PYRAMIDS

Of mummies both mysterious and magical.
Be still: ponder those wonders on a sail down the Nile.

PART III

Going Off-Grid

The Joy of Getting Your Nose Out of Your Phone

It's no longer a surprise to anyone that our smart phones, real-time alert watches, fitness bands, virtual assistants, and social media apps are making us feel anxious, guilty, less productive, and more than a little narcissistic. But with a steady stream of breaking news alarms, live streams, text pings, and reply-alls, it's impossible to really get away from it all.

Or is it?

Some people can self-moderate, go cold turkey, or make their assistants manage their digital lives. Normal people, on the other hand, the kind without the iron will to resist one last Twitter scroll before bed, may need a bit more hand-holding in the form of a service or experience wherein unplugging is necessary, or even mandatory.

Who would have thought that cellular dead zones, spotty wifi connections, and other obstacles that keep people from being digitally distracted could be so ... enticing? When a total digital detox is necessary, sometimes it's best to just get off the grid.

Relinquishing all that hardware not only ensures the sweet sound of silent devices but also a heightened sensitivity to nature. Being unplugged from the incessant demands of the digital world is the essence of vacation.

Not surprisingly, the places we gravitate toward are usually located in spectacular natural landscapes and offer accommodations and environments that encourage reflection, relaxation, and recharging with physical activities, good food, spa treatments, and plenty of alone time. No one can counter societal excesses as effectively as Mother Nature.

Side effects of traveling this way will most certainly include dopamine boosts, increased mindfulness, a better appreciation of one's environment, and a general sense of awe. In no particular order, here are the best places we know to go to unplug.

Opposite page: Sunset on Petit St. Vincent, Caribbean; this page: riding along the beach in Patagonia Austral Marine National Park in Argentina; overleaf page, left: nearly deserted Quirpon Island, Newfoundland; overleaf page, right: a secluded retreat in the Umbrian woods of Terni, Italy

FUN FACT: The Labrador Retriever can trace its ancestry back to Newfoundland and Labrador, the easternmost province in Canada. Labs were originally bred and used as working dogs for fishermen. In addition to being utterly lovable, they're also strong swimmers and loyal rescue animals.

POLAR AND PERFECT: QUIRPON LIGHTHOUSE INN
Quirpon Island, Newfoundland, Canada

In the far reaches of the North Atlantic, in Canada's easternmost province, the remote islands of Newfoundland offer outstanding glimpses of Arctic life – puffins, icebergs, polar bears – from their rocky shores. For a rustic, old-fashioned, seafaring-themed weekend, travelers can head further out to Quirpon Island, a deserted spit of land reachable via a five-hour drive from the city of Deer Lake and a coordinated private boat transfer, where a lighthouse has been converted into a cozy, rustic, ten-room inn operating from the end of May through the third week in September. Because of its location, there is virtually no cellular service and certainly no wifi. But there are frolicking foxes, berry foraging expeditions, a centuries-old settlement guests can hike to, and zodiacs and kayaks for iceberg viewing (Quirpon is the province's best location for taking them in). The real stars of the island are its 27 species of whale, including humpback, minke, and orca. Seeing the great creatures is practically inevitable, and the inn encourages guests to settle into the heated, indoor whale-watching station with a good book and a cup of tea while listening out for whale songs.

linkumtours.com
+1 877 254 6586

ISOLATION IN ITALY: EREMITO
Parrano, Umbria, Italy

Entrepreneur Marcello Murzilli spent four years planning and building his modern-day monastery, the better to serve his vision of an environmentally conscious sanctuary safe from the digital age. The 21-room retreat, built stone by stone using ancient masonry techniques, is nestled in an Umbrian hillside, a 90-minute drive from Rome, and goes to great lengths to simplify life as we know it. It's a new kind of travel experience made specifically for the solo traveler: there is no internet, no minibar, no television. A gong sounds nightly at 8pm, signaling the start of silent dinner, which is sourced from the garden and nearby farms and served in a refectory-style dining room; illumination is mostly by candlelight. There's breakfast and lunch, daily yoga and meditation, a stone grotto with a hot tub and steam bath, and a beautiful pastoral landscape all around. 'Eremito' means 'hermit' in Italian, a reminder to look within and channel that inner recluse.

eremito.com
Località Tarina 2
+39 0763 891010

INACCESSIBLE ALASKA: SHELDON CHALET
Denali National Park, Alaska, U.S.A.

For much of the 1950s, the mountaineer and surveyor Don Sheldon and his pioneering wife, Roberta, explored and mapped parts of the Alaska Range in what was then called the Territory of Alaska. They registered a claim for a 4.9-acre (2-hectare) parcel of land, an isolated peak of rock projecting above a large expanse of snow 10 miles (16 kilometers) from the summit of Denali, under the Trade Headquarters section of the *Homestead Act*. A generation later, the Sheldon kids opened a homey and high-end five-bedroom glacial island lodge, accessible only by helicopter or plane. A stay here is about viewing nature in its extreme, as the hexagonal chalet has panoramic views of pristine snow and sparkling glaciers that go on for miles. Data, cell coverage, and internet connectivity do not exist. (The on-site guides, chef, and concierge use a radio to communicate with the outside world.) Every single piece of lumber, every drawer pull, and every Alaskan King Crab leg is flown in via a tiny airstrip established by the elder Sheldon. There are no people, few animals, and little vegetation. Just peaceful silence and incredibly fresh air. Up to ten guests can stay at a time, sharing locally sourced meals, swinging on hammocks, cozying up in front of the fireplace, and taking advantage of a bevy of excursions: glacier trekking, skiing, rappelling, heli-fishing for local salmon, flying over a mastodon bone yard, picnicking on Alaskan charcuterie and foraged foods in an igloo, and visiting remote hot springs. Nightly shows include meteor showers, ice blizzards, avalanches, and unfettered views of the aurora borealis.

sheldonchalet.com
+1 907 854 7007

Things You Can Do Without Looking at Your Phone: A Checklist

- [ ] Learn chess
- [ ] Fly a kite
- [ ] People watch
- [ ] Build a bonfire
- [ ] Have real conversations with strangers
- [ ] Sketch what you see in a notebook
- [ ] Gamble
- [ ] Practice a two-fingered whistle
- [ ] Press flowers
- [ ] Train a falcon
- [ ] Float on your back
- [ ] Bake a loaf of bread

CARIBBEAN REVERIE: PETIT ST. VINCENT
St. Vincent and the Grenadines, Caribbean

After flying to Barbados, taking a puddle jumper to Union Island, and hopping a boat to come ashore on this little-known Caribbean island (referred to as PSV), the outside world will be a distant memory. Part of the reason the tiny island resort is so perfect is because it's hard to reach. There's a strictly unplugged-luxury vibe, which has been partly cultivated and partly left alone for the last 50 years, as the resort teeters on being a wholly sustainable operation. Guests of the 22 simple oceanfront cottages have access to pristine private beaches, impeccable service, and the Jean-Michel Cousteau Caribbean Diving Center (jeanmichelcousteaudiving-caribbean. com). It says something about the quality of the snorkeling and diving there that Cousteau picked PSV over hundreds of other islands dotting the Caribbean.

No locks, no clocks, no TVs, and no wireless in the rooms. There are landlines in the main office and, depending on the weather, you might find a lingering cell signal from a neighboring island, but the idea here is to completely disconnect. Guests can walk, bike, or hitch a ride in a little Mini Moke car. A flag system is used at each cabin to communicate with staff – a red flag means do not disturb; a yellow flag means the guest has a request. Meals are local, fresh-caught, and may be served in your room or the beach restaurant (sand floors, no shoes required). The spa is built into the hillside, with wooden pathways leading to treatment rooms overlooking the water. Kayaking, sailing, and catching the sunrise after a restful sleep are all on the agenda.

petitstvincent.com
+1 800 654 9326

Opposite page, top: Coming in for a landing at Sheldon Chalet; opposite page, bottom: viewing the aurora borealis; this page, top: underwater pal found in the clear waters off Petit St. Vincent; this page, middle: a waterfront view; this page, bottom: playing around; overleaf page: Alphonse Island, Seychelles

REMOTE SEYCHELLES:
ALPHONSE ISLAND
Outer Islands, Seychelles

The ultimate getaway vacation is a pristine, private island resort 250 miles (402 kilometers) south-west of Mahé, the capital of the Seychelles, and a long way from the African mainland. Needless to say, there's no wifi in the rooms and no cell service at all, but with everything that's available on this unspoiled dot in the middle of the Indian Ocean, what reason will you have to phone for anything? Among many watersports and wildlife-viewing opportunities, there are giant tortoises to meet, turtles to track, spinner dolphins to swim with, game fish to hook, saltwater fly-fishing to try, and coral reefs to explore. (Alphonse is the only one of the Outer Islands to offer scuba diving. The others are uninhabited.) Accommodations include 22 private bungalows and five suites, each air-conditioned and equipped with private bicycles, outdoor showers, and easy access to the island's ubiquitous white-sand beaches, which you'll be spending all of your sunsets on, if you're not on a catamaran drinking cocktails at sea.

alphonse-island.com
+27 82 496 4570

FUN FACT: Look to Central and South America for a sheer abundance of nature. Patagonia, an enormous expanse of desert, glaciers, and rainforest, has a nearly one to one ratio of people to penguins. Nicaragua has 0.01 per cent of the world's land mass but 7 per cent of its biodiversity.

PATAGONIAN NATURE OVERLOAD: BAHIA BUSTAMANTE LODGE

Patagonia, Argentina

Not that you'd want to sit around checking emails when you have a sustainable sheep farm, an island full of Magellanic penguins, and a 60-million-year-old petrified forest nearby, but at this former Patagonian seaweed settlement– turned–seaside eco-lodge, you really don't have the choice. There's no cell phone service and electricity is only available in the evenings, during which time the wifi offered in the lobby is spotty at best. The beautifully restored cabins, which used to house settlement workers and their families, don't have TVs either. All the better to help you focus on why you trekked down here in the first place – to revel in the natural beauty and biodiversity of the area's beaches, bluffs, and farmland. Part of Patagonia Austral Marine National Park and UNESCO's Patagonia Azul Biosphere Reserve, the grounds are teeming with wildlife – sea lions, rare birds, armadillos, and guanacos included – which guests can observe on a number of bike rides, treks, and tours organized according to the day's weather conditions.

bahiabustamante.com
9111 Comodoro Rivadavia
+ 54 9 11 4156 7788

NICARAGUA'S CLOUD FOREST ESCAPE: FINCA ESPERANZA VERDE

San Ramón, Matagalpa, Nicaragua

Nestled in a cloud forest in the mountains, this verdant eco-lodge and working organic coffee farm gives visitors a chance to become immersed in a different pace of life. Rooms are rustic and have no electrical outlets – just hammocks and sweeping hundred-mile views – and wifi is only available in the dining area. There's only one charging station in the library, so don't expect to meet any deadlines here. Everything runs on solar and hydroelectric power (and wood fires, for the showers and bread ovens), and the mountain water is so clean it's been officially certified as safe to drink. The delicious food comes from an on-site organic farm tended to by a veteran farmer who plants based on the cycles of the moon and the position of the stars.

Your days are spent in the butterfly garden, hiking to waterfalls along several different trails, birdwatching, and at nightly folkloric jam sessions around the bonfire. As for alarm clocks, the howler monkeys will take care of waking you up. The finca (ranch) makes a concerted effort to empower the staff – most of whom live within a 2.5-mile (4-kilometer) radius of the farm and belong to the rural community of La Chispa – by discussing new projects with them and encouraging them to feel a sense of pride in running the farm. The owners even help support an elementary school for 45 of the community's kids on the property and run a cultural exchange, giving guests the opportunity to interact with locals in their own homes.

fincaesperanzaverde.com
+505 8 775 5341

WESTERN AUSTRALIA SEASIDE: SAL SALIS NINGALOO REEF
Cape Range National Park, Western Australia

A safari camp. On the beach. Bordering the world's largest coral reef that you can swim to from the shore. With no internet access or cell phone reception whatsoever. Call it the ultimate digital detox. With all the extra headspace, guests can pick and choose their adventure. Guided bush walks let you explore the outback of Cape Range National Park, a rugged limestone range dotted with caves and dramatic gorges; critters like emus, wallabies, and red kangaroo; and a variety of flora endemic to the area, which used to be its own island eons ago. Seaside excursions within Ningaloo Marine Park allow guests to swim with whale sharks, humpbacks, and dolphins, kayak among sea turtles, and snorkel through coral lagoons. After retreating to one of 15 luxury tents and indulging in exceptional Western Australian food and wine, guests only need to look up at one of the best expressions of the Milky Way to cap off a day at one with nature.

salsalis.com.au
Cape Range National Park, Exmouth, WA
+61 8 9949 1776

OOTO IN THE MALDIVES: SONEVA FUSHI
Baa Atoll, The Maldives

Nothing will stress you out when you're gazing out at the horizon from your own luxurious villa on a private island hideaway in one of the most beautiful stretches of wide-open ocean in the world. But if you're prone to distraction of the digital sort, there are steps you can take to stay disconnected. In addition to luxurious amenities like pools, wine fridges, and steam rooms, each villa comes with a switch that toggles the wifi. Common areas lack internet connection altogether, allowing guests to ground themselves fully in spa treatments, musical instrument lessons, cocktail-making classes, arts and crafts with the kids, film screenings under the stars, and a variety of carefully executed dining experiences. If you really need to get away from it all, hop on a boat for a free-diving excursion, to a nearby sandbank for an overnight glamping experience in a Bedouin-style tent, or to an uninhabited island for a luxurious Maldivian dinner at an 18-seat beach restaurant.

soneva.com
Kunfunadhoo Island
+960 660 0304

HEALTH AND WELLNESS: VILLA STÉPHANIE
Baden-Baden, Germany

The famous spa town in south-west Germany's Black Forest has been drawing elite travelers in need of holistic pampering at its old Roman baths since the Belle Époque. Villa Stéphanie, an elegant 15-bedroom mansion and destination spa adjacent to 145-year-old five-star Brenners Park-Hotel, is a no-expense-spared affair for the digital detoxer: the inner walls of the home are outfitted with a copper grid that allows guests to switch off all wireless communication simply by pressing a bedside button. With all that digital pollution gone, travelers can pay careful attention to the architectural heritage of the space, including the beautiful vestibules, marble bathrooms, wrought-iron balconies, gentlemanly library, and pristine Loro Piana fabrics. The nearly 54,000-square-foot (5017-square-meter) spa is part futuristic medical clinic and part old-world hammam (with sauna, plunge pool, thermal suite, and private gym). There are detoxing programs galore for ailments of all kinds and state-of-the-art medical care from experts in physiotherapy, dentistry, ophthalmology, and more. Nutritionists tailor dining menus to guests' needs and set up full programs for the length of everyone's stay. After a blissful massage and a night free from social media, the thought of an early morning walk through the private gardens, a water aerobics class, and a hike in the mountains feels not so much like a boot camp but rather a healthy lifestyle shift.

oetkercollection.com
Schillerstraße 4/6
+49 7221 900 602
Spa hours: 8am–8pm

This page: Western Australia's coast; overleaf page: exploring the Northern Territory's floodplains in Australia

AT THE EDGE OF THE WORLD: BAMURRU PLAINS
Top End, Northern Territory, Australia

You'll be freed from internet, wifi, and mobile coverage on the coastal floodplains of Australia's Top End. This is bush country, where, from May to October, the land turns into a temporary water world ready for full days of safari exploration. Ten stylish safari bungalows powered by the sun have mesh walls on three sides, allowing guests to feel the wilderness all around. At sunrise, airboats skim across the floodplains in search of blue-winged kookaburra, magpie geese, and slinky crocodiles (the area is home to the largest density of crocodiles in the world). On dry land, days are spent in open-top trucks, on quad bikes, and on walks in search of wallabies, buffalo, wild horses, and an incredible array of rare birds. Once you've gone offline, you may find that you feel best doing nothing more than lazing around in the infinity pool, snacking on bush-tucker canapés, and hitting up the self-service bar. Dinner is a three-course affair highlighting low-impact local produce and game.

bamurruplains.com
Mary River Floodplain, Kakadu
+61 2 9571 6399

Into the Wild:
Follow Their Lead

These off-grid group trips and expeditions are not the kind of thing you want to bring your high-maintenance pal on, since there will be physical labor, composting toilets, and the occasional cold shower. But the memories, landscapes, and cultural exchanges are breathtaking and unforgettable.

JOIN A RUSSIAN REINDEER EXPEDITION
Russia and Siberia

Intrepid, the veteran global adventure company, offers an offbeat 15-day adventure not for the faint of heart or mind. The small group trip of four to twelve people begins in St. Petersburg with a wifi-free, 47-hour train ride (25 on the Trans-Polar Railway), bus adventure, and Russian six-wheeled amphibious all-terrain vehicle joy-ride to reach well beyond the Arctic Circle, to the Yamal Peninsula, where travelers are welcomed into a tribe of nomadic reindeer herders called the Nenets. Reindeer sledding, fishing, and snowmobiling on the frozen tundra ensues. Not to mention camaraderie with the nomads and learning life-saving tricks, like how to stay warm in -50˚F (-46˚C) weather.

Good to know: No flushing toilets, no cell service, and no wifi. 'Roughing it' might be an understatement.

intrepidtravel.com

FUN FACT: Recent studies have revealed a 'wanderlust gene' — a genetic derivative of DRD4, which is associated with the dopamine levels in the brain and correlate to increased levels of curiosity, risk, and restlessness.

Opposite page: Soneva Fushi sandbank in the spectacular Maldives; this page: a rugged road-trip vehicle for Arctic adventuring

SLUMBER IN A FIELD OF LIGHTNING
New Mexico, U.S.A.

Life imitates art in this off-the-grid installation in a mysterious desert location in New Mexico's Catron County, 7200 feet (2195 meters) above sea level. A group of up to six are picked up at a designated place and driven to a cabin in an undisclosed location to take part in an overnight experience of Land Art by the American sculptor Walter De Maria. The Lightning Field consists of 400 polished stainless-steel poles stretched across the high desert, a grid measuring 1 mile by 0.6 miles (1.6 kilometres × 1 kilometre). Visitors are encouraged to walk around the field, especially during sunset and sunrise, whether there's a lightning storm or not, to take in the mind-altering effect of the sun's rays on the metal poles and the charred earth from lightning strikes. Back at the cabin, simple meals and lodging are provided, along with books and an emergency phone. No other devices allowed.

Good to know: Visiting slots have filled up quickly since the launch of the work in 1977. Book early and pack sturdy shoes.

diaart.org
+1 505 898 3335

GO BACK TO GROUND ZERO AT THE RANCH
Malibu, California, U.S.A

Go back to hardcore basics in pursuit of a healthy mind, body, and soul. The sprawling 1920s hacienda-style estate, a former summer camp, sits on 100-plus acres (40-plus hectares) and has been transformed into 14 well-appointed private cabins with common areas, indoor and outdoor dining areas, two workout facilities, and a year-round organic farm. There is no cell service and wifi is limited to in-room use. You should make this an unplugged boot camp for personal excavation. Plus, you'll need to pay attention to your hydration needs while taking a mega hike or holding a sunrise chaturanga. Depending on which program you opt into, days will be filled with fitness regimes, wellness support, and a monastic meal plan.

Good to know: Sustainability is key in maintaining a healthy lifestyle, and whether you visit the ranch for four, seven, or ten days, the journey begins 30 days prior with a series of suggested exercises, dietary restrictions, and living assignments to prepare you for the mega detoxing on site.

theranchmalibu.com
12220 Cotharin Road
+1 310 457 8700

Opposite page: The Great Room at The Ranch at Live Oak; this page, top: night sky in New Mexico; this page, bottom: hiking around Malibu, California

Join a Russian reindeer expedition with Intrepid Travel

SPEND THE NIGHT IN A SKYBED IN THE OKAVANGO DELTA
Khwai Private Reserve, Botswana

Two lodges in the middle of the African wilderness can be combined for a multi-night sleeping adventure through the Natural Selection safari group. Skybeds camp is comprised of three-story rustic platforms in the trees overlooking a watering hole frequented by giraffes, wildebeest, and elephants. After a night or two spent close to the stars, travelers can move to sister camp Sable Alley, a more luxurious (but no more technologically connected) lagoonside tented accommodation with an Afro-chic indoor seating area, double bed, and writing desk for recording animal sightings and feelings of awe.

Good to know: Invite your friends. The camp can accommodate parties of up to six people. (Just no children under the age of 12.)

naturalselection.travel
+27 210 011 574

PADDLE TO YOUR HEART'S CONTENT IN THE FROZEN OCEAN CANOE TREK
Kejimkujik National Park, Nova Scotia, Canada

A real get-your-hands-dirty camping experience. Whynot Adventure leads three-day backcountry expeditions on canoes to different campsites, allowing travelers to experience the wilderness of this eastern Canada maritime province. Paddlers are given a tent, camping equipment, easy-to-make dishes, and freshly ground coffee each morning. Days are spent moving from picturesque lakes and rivers that connect lovely campsites, a neat experience for adventurous families and groups of friends.

Good to know: The experience is only for those who are up to and capable of physical activity for multiple hours.

whynotadventure.ca
+1 902 682 2282

Opposite page: Basecamp in Greenland; this page, top: the night sky in Botswana; this page, middle: canoe paddles for a frozen ocean trek; this page, bottom: the calm waters of Canada

SLEEP ON AN ICE SHEET
Greenland

Natural Habitat Adventures' deluxe safari-style camp near the edge of the Greenland ice sheet is one of the most isolated places on Earth. Up to 12 guests can experience remote areas that very few have ever seen. The area, once inaccessible except by kayak, is now the only luxury basecamp in the country. Feel the cool breeze off massive icebergs and keep your eyes peeled for whales. Rub elbows with local Inuit in their fishing villages. Evening lectures are presented by Arctic naturalists who double as guides. As there's no wifi or cell service, you'll have to save sharing adventures and pictures for when you get home.

Good to know: Environmental sustainability is a highly important aspect of traveling through the rapidly changing Arctic and other habitats threatened by climate change. The emissions from the trip are 100 per cent carbon-offset by Natural Habitat, the world's first carbon-neutral travel company.

nathab.com
U.S.A. and Canada: +1 800 543 8917;
International: +1 303 449 3711

LIFE-CHANGING TIP #03

Feels Like the Middle of Nowhere

Some of our favorite accommodations are up to speed on 21st-century technology, but make unplugging a better alternative.

EXPLORA RAPA NUI
Easter Island, Chile
Serious stone faces. Ocean views. Expert-led expeditions.
explora.com

HÓTEL BÚÐIR
Snæfellsnæs Peninsula, Iceland
Puffins as neighbors. Locally sourced meals. Lava fields and northern lights.
hotelbudir.is

TIERRA ATACAMA HOTEL & SPA
San Pedro de Atacama, Chile
Stargaze from sand dunes and geysers, hot springs, and horseback.
tierrahotels.com

SOUTHERN OCEAN LODGE
Kangaroo Island, South Australia
Animals galore and nothing else between your patio and Antarctica.
southernoceanlodge.com.au

AMANGIRI
Canyon Point, Utah, U.S.A.
Navajo-inspired desert marvel. Stark and striking.
aman.com

TAPROBANE ISLAND
Weligama Bay, Sri Lanka
A legendary mansion accessible by wading through the sea or crossing by elephant.
taprobaneisland.com

FOGO ISLAND INN
Fogo Island, Newfoundland, Canada
Raw and beautiful coast. Centuries-old island culture. Alive and well.
fogoislandinn.ca

THREE CAMEL LODGE
Southern Gobi Desert, Mongolia
Fantastic ger camp next door to 5000-year-old petroglyphs.
threecamellodge.com

TAKE A RUGGED KIMBERLEY COAST CRUISE
The Kimberley, Western Australia
Coral Expeditions' Australian-flagged fleet of three rugged ships was purpose-built for exploration. The Kimberley coast cruise requires a minimum of ten nights and brings passengers on a full tour of the ancient, hard-to-access region from April through September. Expect waterfalls, ancient art sites, and expert interpretation of landscape, nature, wildlife, and history. Covering over 154,440 square miles (400,000 square kilometers), the land is only home to 30,000 people, making it one of the largest areas of unfettered wilderness in the world.

Good to know: This is much more intimate than a standard cruise ship, which is part of the charm. There are three styles of ship, all varying slightly in shape and size. The largest accommodates 120 guests and the smallest only 44.

coralexpeditions.com
+61 7 4040 9999

Opposite page, top: Coral Expeditions rafting excursion; opposite page, bottom: a walking safari; this page: waterfalls in Western Australia

WALK ON THE WILD SIDE IN ZAMBIA
South Luangwa National Park, Zambia

A pioneer of the guided walking safari, Robin Pope has been leading small groups into the African wilderness for decades. On this seven-day trek, guests cover about 6 miles (10 kilometers) on foot per day along the Mupamadzi River, with guides setting up a full-service, portable camp at each day's end. Travelers pad lightly in search of elephants, leopards, buffalo, rare birds, and giraffes, with local guides skilled in navigating on foot.

Good to know: Meals (and wine) are provided on portable dining tables with tablecloths. Full bedding is set up under walk-in tents lit by lanterns and the moon. The experience is luxurious despite being totally cut off from technology and indoor showers. The shower is under a tree and the toilet, if you're wondering, is a bush loo with a wooden throne.

robinpopesafaris.net
+265 0 999 970 002

PART IV

The World's Best Escapes for Foodies

Go Ahead, Eat Your Heart Out

If you travel for the food, you're not alone. Welcome to this happy band of travelers who plan dinner when we're sitting at lunch, who think nothing of driving four hours for that dinner, and, in fact, would plan a whole trip around that meal.

For us, the world's best culinary escapes have to be more than amazing hotels with even better restaurants. Much more. We want unforgettable, meal-of-a-lifetime culinary immersions. The kind of travel experiences where guests can live the farm-to-table life by staying on a working farm or winery and seeing and participating in the steps that lead to those spectacular plates getting to the table. Where activities between meals include foraging expeditions, wine tastings, cooking lessons, and next-level snacking. Where it's no surprise to see someone in chef whites running out of the kitchen to pick a few last-minute vegetables before dinner.

These foodie escapes around the world are pilgrimages for people who truly care about food – and are maybe more than a little obsessed with their palates. Some of these illustrious culinary experiences have a price tag to match, others mix high and low, and a few are downright affordable. All of these special occasions will make you very hungry and leave you very satisfied.

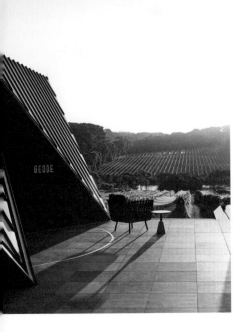

Opposite page: Lime Wood Hotel in Lyndhurst, England; this page, top: apples from SingleThread Farm in Healdsburg, California; this page, bottom: Jackalope on the Mornington Peninsula outside of Melbourne, Australia

SINGLETHREAD
Healdsburg, California, U.S.A.

What we love: At the junction of Russian River, Dry Creek, and Alexander Valley – three of Sonoma County's principal wine regions – sits Healdsburg, a charming small-town home to some of northern California's best wine and cuisine. Topping the list is SingleThread, a two-Michelin-star farm, restaurant, and inn, where chef Kyle Connaughton and his wife, Katina, are redefining farm-to-table seasonality. Drawing upon ancient Japanese gardening techniques, the 11-course menu, which opens with a dazzling display of amuse-bouches that are at the table when guests are seated, rotates not around four seasons but rather 72 distinct micro-seasons, guaranteeing that the food grown on their 5-acre (2-hectare) farm (and on the restaurant's rooftop) is only served at its peak freshness. The ensuing meal, prepared in and served upon earthenware imported directly from eighth-generation master potters in Japan, is as spectacular as this level of precision, ingenuity, and dedication would lead you to expect. Spend the night upstairs in one of the inn's five well-appointed guest rooms to experience Japanese hospitality, or 'omotenashi', at its finest.
House specialty: Whatever's in (micro)season.

singlethreadfarms.com
+1 707 723-4646
Dinner from 5.30pm, weekend lunch from 11.30am

LIME WOOD
Lyndhurst, England

What we love: Located two hours outside London, deep in the heart of New Forest, a national park and former royal hunting ground, this 13th-century lodge-turned-resort is the embodiment of every urbanite's dream escape to the British countryside. The on-site restaurant, Hartnett Holder & Co, is led by two of London's most celebrated chefs, Angela Hartnett and Luke Holder. The menu relies heavily on local ingredients, many foraged from the surrounding woods, resulting in an understated yet refined blend of British and Italian cuisine. The cooking school, HH&Co Backstage, is designed to instruct aspiring chefs of all skill levels in the art of Hartnett and Holder's signature homestyle cooking.
House specialty: The fillings in the pillow-like agnolotti change seasonally to showcase star ingredients sourced nearby – guinea fowl, veal, artichokes, and burrata.

limewoodhotel.co.uk
Beaulieu Road
+44 23 8028 7177
12–2.30pm, 6–10pm

Opposite page: Jackalope's bold and modern architecture; this page, top: The restaurant at SingleThread; this page, bottom: dishes from Hartnett Holder & Co. at Lime Wood

JACKALOPE HOTEL
Merricks North, Victoria, Australia

What we love: Located in the heart of the Mornington Peninsula wine region an hour south of Melbourne, the 45-room luxury hotel is a veritable food and design destination. Look no further than the surrounding oceanside vineyard, the club-like cocktail bar in an old Edwardian homestead decorated in Rick Owens furniture, and the 23-foot (7-meter) namesake jackalope statue out front – and you'll have an idea why. There are two farm-to-fork restaurants, multi-course degustation menus that lean heavily on local produce, and gastro excursions like Truffle Trinity, where guests head out to look for black truffles with a local expert and her dog, culminating in a celebratory fungus feast with wine pairings.
House specialty: The ever-changing, five-course tasting menu at Doot Doot Doot is a showstopper, pairing artfully prepared Mornington Peninsula produce with wines from vineyards under 27 acres (11 hectares) in size.

jackalopehotels.com
166 Balnarring Road
+61 3 5931 2500
Sunday–Thursday dinner from 6.30pm; Friday and Saturday dinner from 6pm; Saturday and Sunday lunch from 12.30–2pm

LIFE-CHANGING TIP #04

Bites Worth the Distance

Delicate, local, abundant Te Matuku oysters.
The Oyster Inn, Waiheke Island, New Zealand
theoysterinn.co.nz

Russian pancakes served in a pool of real maple syrup.
Arthurs Nosh Bar, Montreal, Canada
arthursmtl.com

A divine porchetta (pork) sandwich served on chewy ciriola bread.
Er Buchetto, Rome, Italy
Via del Viminale, 2F
+39 329 965 2175

Cheese-stuffed hibiscus flowers (or apricots, or peppers, the list goes on).
Yom Tov Delicatessen, Tel Aviv, Israel
Levinsky 43
+972 54 682 2020

A salad of raw kale, sea vegetables, avocado, teriyaki almonds, and tahini dressing.
Cafe Gratitude, Los Angeles, California, U.S.A.
cafegratitude.com

Noodles, pork, and local greens in the regional dish cao làu.
Miss Ly Cafe, Hoi An, Vietnam
22 Nguyen Hue Street
+84 235 3861 603

Handmade tagliatelle drenched in black truffles.
Del Ponte, Scheggino, Italy
hoteldelpontescatolini.it

Better-than-gran's Scotch eggs.
The Hind's Head, Bray, England
hindsheadbray.com

Fresh-from-the-garden tomato and asparagus sandwich.
São Lourenço do Barrocal, Portugal
barrocal.pt

Not-too-fancy fish and chips (haddock, tempura batter, homemade tartar sauce).
Fishy Fishy, Kinsale, Ireland
fishyfishy.ie

Tart and perfect lemongrass soufflé in a lemon half.
Cafe Grey Deluxe, Hong Kong
upperhouse.com

12-ingredient, chocolate-free (gasp!) mole poblano.
Augurio, Puebla, Mexico
augurio.mx

Oven-roasted oysters.
Cochon, New Orleans, Louisiana, U.S.A.
cochonrestaurant.com

Spaghetti vongole macchiato.
Lo Scoglio da Tommaso, Amalfi Coast, Italy
hotelloscoglio.com

Perfectly messy falafel sandwich.
L'As du Fallafel
32–34 Rue des Rosiers, Paris, France
+33 1 48 87 63 60

Rich and savory trahana (lamb-stock porridge), after a heavy night of drinking.
Mitos, Athens, Greece
62 Aristeidou Street

Fluffy, cornmeal-dusted English muffins.
Model Bakery, Napa, California, U.S.A.
themodelbakery.com

Tapas-style aubergines with labne and chimichurri sauce.
Yudale, Jerusalem, Israel
Beit Ya'akov Street 11
+972 2 533 3442

Lemon-buttery shrimp scampi with a side of caramelized garlic–topped rice.
Giovanni's Shrimp Truck, Kahuku, Oahu, Hawaii, U.S.A.
giovannisshrimptruck.com

Italian sausage and beef topped with pickled veggies and stuffed into French bread.
Johnnie's Beef, Elmwood Park, Illinois, U.S.A.
500 W North Avenue
+1 708 452 6000

Dan tat, the most classic egg custard tart.
Tai Cheong Bakery, Hong Kong
taoheung.com.hk

Clam chowder in a sourdough bread bowl, eaten dockside.
Tognazzini, San Luis Obispo, California, U.S.A.
morrobaydockside.com

Super-savory, extra peppery, pasta alla gricia (pork and pecorino to the max).
La Tavernaccia, Rome, Italy
latavernacciaroma.com

Famed brioche toast with house-made ricotta and seasonal jam.
Sqirl, Los Angeles, California, U.S.A.
sqirlla.com

Elaborate Japanese bento box breakfast.
Aman Tokyo, Tokyo, Japan
aman.com

Finger-lickin' jerk chicken and pork with house sauce.
Scotchies, Falmouth Road, Montego Bay, Jamaica
+1 876 953 8041

Authentic Jersey-style tomato pie pizza.
Delorenzo's, Robbinsville, New Jersey, U.S.A.
delorenzostomatopies.com

Airy cheese soufflé, followed by chocolate soufflé.
L'Auberge Bressane, Paris, France
auberge-bressane.com

FUN FACT: We are not only what we eat but how we eat. Japanese dining etiquette holds that chopsticks should never be used to pass food to someone else, nor to spear food. And never, ever lick them.

GARZÓN EL HOTEL
Garzón, Uruguay

What we love: In this remote, rural Uruguayan village, world-renowned Argentine chef Francis Mallmann – a man as famous for creating an empire around natural, open-air grilling as he is for his eccentric culinary persona – decided to open a hotel and restaurant. Like any Mallmann venture, it brings the heat. Menu items like 'bread on the coals' and 'burnt fruits' are a testament to his particular style of cooking, in which fire – the earth oven, grill, and fire stoves in the kitchen all burn wood – is used to bring out the strongest and most natural flavors in every ingredient. The hotel, in what used to be Garzón's general store, resembles a quaint, provincial country home. And, yes, every room has its own fireplace, too.

House specialty: The ribeye with chimichurri and domino potatoes, tomato, and scallion on the coals. This is cowboy country, after all.

restaurantegarzon.com
Costa Jose Ignacio
+598 4410 2809
9am–11pm

FÄVIKEN
Jämtland, Sweden

What we love: Swedish chef Magnus Nilsson and his dedicated staff forage, garden, and hunt on 20,000 acres (8094 hectares) of farmland and wilderness 466 miles (750 kilometers) north of Stockholm. Then comes the hard work of preserving, pickling, and preparing everything (except for salt and sugar) for the meals they serve (including 32 outrageous dinner courses) to two dozen diners in an old barn. Guests, for their part, have to schlep to this hinterland, where they then sauna out the northern chill and give their stomachs over completely to the kitchen for a high-context meal that brings them back down to Earth. Five simple rooms – wood slabs make up the floors, walls, and ceiling – are decorated with fur throws and sprays of pine boughs and dried wildflowers. After dinner, a roaring fire in a teepee serves as a snug for those who want a nightcap and to talk about the incredible farmhouse breakfast to come.

House specialty: Nilsson often refers to the 'simplified complexity and deliciousness' of locally harvested scallops cooked over juniper and birch charcoal and served in their shells.

favikenmagasinet.se
Fäviken 216
+46 0647 401 77

This page: In the kitchen at chef Magnus Nilsson's Faviken; overleaf page: a beautiful dish at Babylonstoren

BABYLONSTOREN
Franschhoek, South Africa

What we love: Located an hour outside Cape Town in the Franschhoek wine valley, this farm is one of the oldest and best preserved examples of Cape Dutch farmland. The 8-acre (3.5-hectare) garden at the heart of the farm grows everything from waterblommetjies, edible flowers, to several varieties of prickly pear. The garden's bounties are served in the three restaurants, Babel, Greenhouse, and Bakery, reflecting the farm's 'pick, clean, and serve' philosophy. The garden plays host to several hands-on workshops every month, or guests can tour the estate's wine cellar and drink away the day in the tasting room. The suites and cottages, set adjacent to the garden, all feel like part of an elegant, contemporary country home.

House specialty: The green, red, or yellow salad, an assortment of fruits and vegetables (arranged by color) picked from the garden daily.

babylonstoren.com
Klapmuts Simondium Road
+27 21 863 3852
Monday–Sunday: breakfast from 8–9.30am, dinner from 7pm;
Wednesday–Sunday, lunch from 12pm

Opposite page: Tending the garden at Le Manior; this page, top left: a delicious dish from the onsite restaurant; top right: a view of Monachyle Mhor; this page, bottom left: scenic Scottish lochs; this page, bottom right: the rugged Scottish countryside

MONACHYLE MHOR
Loch Lomond and The Trossachs National Park, Scotland

What we love: The Lewis family–owned, bubble-gum pink, 16-room farmhouse hotel sits on the bonnie banks of lochs Voil and Doine, an easy two-hour drive from Edinburgh. The on-site restaurant, run by philosopher-chef Tom Lewis, is superb – think elevated dining in a cozy home setting. But there's plenty to gawk at before sitting down for a meal. After all, there are lakes full of fish, distilleries full of single malt, and a 2000-acre (809-hectare) sustainable farm full of animals to keep you wandering. At informal cooking classes at the inn, guests may learn to cook, shuck, and fillet while enjoying a wee dram. Off property, the empire includes motel–restaurant Mhor 84 and the cute boutique Mhor in Store. Farther down the road in Callander are Mhor Bread, the 100-year-old bakery for loaves of sourdough (Scottish milled flour only), and Mhor Fish, the fish-and-chippery where potatoes are fried in beef fat.
House specialty: Venison cooked with respect and good butter, foraged chanterelles, and green 'bits and bobs' from the garden.

monachylemhor.net
Balquhidder
+44 1877 384 622
12–2pm, 6.45–9pm

BELMOND LE MANOIR AUX QUAT'SAISONS
Oxfordshire, England

What we love: Le Manoir, which recently became a Belmond property, is an OG farm-to-table experience: it was at the forefront of locavore before it became an overused buzzword, and has maintained two Michelin stars for over 30 years. A short hop from London, it's a global Eden where the chef and menu are French, one garden is Japanese, the croquet pitch is British, and the pampered guests feel connected to Mother Earth. The 32-room hotel is at once sumptuous and cozy; the meals are refined and fresh. The cookery school offers a wide range of topics (summer dinner party, patisserie, kitchen secrets) in half- and full-day options, for adults as well as children.

House specialty: Everything from the 2-acre (1-hectare) garden, which produces varieties of 90 vegetables, more than 70 herbs, 20 different mushrooms, and an orchard of apples, pears, and quince.

belmond.com
Church Road
+44 1844 278 881
Dinner 6.30–9.30pm, lunch Tuesday–Sunday 11.45am–2.15pm

Your Bar Order Around the World

What to drink to feel like a local – morning, noon, and night.

Italy: cappuccino, Aperol spritz, negroni

Morocco: orange juice, almond milk (with orange blossom water), mint tea

Jamaica: sorrel (hibiscus) tea, ginger beer, rum

Argentina: cafe con leche, mate, malbec

England: black tea, pint of beer, gin and tonic

Japan: barley tea, matcha, sake

India: chai tea, lassi (yogurt and spices), lemonade with ginger

France: cafe au lait, wine, Champagne

Brazil: pingado (warm milk with coffee), vitaminas (fruit smoothie), caipirinha

Australia: flat white, espresso martini, shiraz

Vietnam: coconut water, sugar cane juice, bia ho'i (local beer)

INN AT SERENBE
Chattahoochee Hills, Georgia, U.S.A.

What we love: This six-building, 27-room hotel is situated on 60 acres (24 hectares), including a 25-acre (10-hectare) organic farm, in Serenbe, a relatively new, progressive, sustainable community on the outskirts of Atlanta that locavores love for its charming, very affordable country-retreat feel. The focus is on regional cuisine – using locally grown, organic ingredients from the restaurant's own garden as well as from Serenbe Farms – which can be sampled in everything from afternoon tea and evening sweets to the full country breakfast, all of which are included in the stay. Chef Brian Moll lives down the road and is known to forage while walking to work at the community's acclaimed restaurant, The Farmhouse.

House specialty: It's the South, so you shouldn't go home without trying the Farmhouse fried chicken, Carolina Gold rice risotto, and bourbon pecan pie.

serenbeinn.com
10950 Hutcheson Ferry Road
+1 770 463 2610
Lunch Saturday and Sunday 11.30am–3pm; dinner Wednesday–Sunday 5–9pm

FUN FACT: While much of wine history is well documented, there is no definitive or really even good reason why large format bottles of wine were named for the biblical kings Jeroboam, Rehoboam, Nebuchadnezzar, and Balthasar.

Opposite page: In bloom at Serenbe; this page, top left: the dining room; this page, top right: fried chicken at Serenbe

Shop Like a Local

Prepare for a feast at our favorite food markets around the world.

	Famous for a Reason	Local Favorite
London	Borough Market	Maltby Street Market
New York City	Union Square Greenmarket	Grand Army Plaza Greenmarket
Barcelona	La Boqueria	Mercado de Santa Caterina
Paris	Marché Bastille	Marché des Enfants Rouges
Seoul	Noryangjin Fish Market	Garak Market
Los Angeles	Santa Monica Farmers' Market	Hollywood Farmers' Market
Rome	Campo de' Fiori	Nuovo Mercato di Testaccio
Seattle	Pike Place Market	Ballard Farmers' Market
Bangkok	Khlong Toei Market	Bang Phli Floating Market
Toronto	St. Lawrence	Leslieville Farmers' Market
Istanbul	Spice Bazaar	Feriköy Organic Market

DON ALFONSO 1890
Sant'Agata sui Due Golfi, Italy

What we love: Italians excel at two things above all else: good taste and warm hospitality, and the Iaccarino family are standouts at both. Their Amalfi Coast compound, located in a town on a hilltop overlooking the Bay of Naples and the Bay of Salerno, is picturesque and charming, with hotel rooms named for herbs and a wine cellar that dates back to the Etruscan era. The only thing more scenic is their vegetable garden on a nearby cliff, which has postcard views of Capri. They'll happily drive you over for a tour – you won't be able to find it otherwise. Save time for a cooking class, because no one should leave without learning to make a Neapolitan pizza.

House specialty: Modern interpretations of classic dishes, wherein cutting-edge techniques and dazzling presentations take fried calamari and zabaglione to new heights.

donalfonso.com
Corso Sant'Agata, 11
+39 081 878 0026
Closed seasonally from November 3 to March 31.
Check the website for hours.

WANÅS RESTAURANT AND HOTEL
Knislinge, Sweden

What we love: Long a destination for art insiders, the stunning 15th-century castle and sculpture park is making a name for itself in the food world with the introduction of a Nordic farm-to-table restaurant and a tastefully designed 11-room sustainable hotel. Located in the countryside a short day trip from Malmö and Copenhagen, the bucolic retreat is a place to connect with nature – in art-filled barns, on the large on-site organic farm, and at the long, communal dining room table.

House specialty: Mushrooms, berries, and flowers foraged from the surrounding beech forest; beef tartare from Wanås's own cows; and soft-serve ice cream made with milk from the organic dairy farm, one of the largest in Europe.

wanasrh.se
Hässleholmsvägen, 289 90 Knislinge
+46 44 253 15 81
10am–7pm, open for dinner for pre-booked guests

Opposite page: Dinner is served at Don Alfonso 1890 on the Amalfi Coast; this page, top: the dining room at Wanås in Sweden; this page, middle: Don Alfonso seen from the pool; bottom: a farm-style building at Wanås

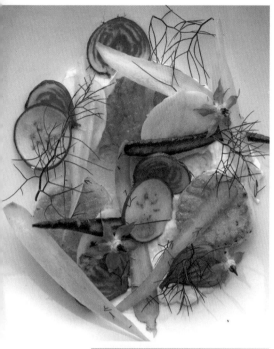

BLACKBERRY FARM
Walland, Tennessee, U.S.A.

What we love: Beautiful rooms. Great spa. Breathtaking Smoky Mountain scenery. Fantastic farm-to-fancy-table cuisine. Regular celebrity chef appearances. And tastings galore (both wine and whiskey). It's the only farm in the U.S. where you're likely to find Italian truffle dogs sniffing under the oak trees and Alice Waters hanging around out back. The retreat is known for its epicurean workshops, daily cooking demonstrations, and wine events, as well as the Farmstead Field School, where guests can take classes like gardening with a master during their stay. (We have even higher hopes for their new property, Blackberry Mountain.)

House specialty: Almost everything – from the cheese, meat, and beer to the mushrooms, blackberries, and ramps – is made or plucked on site. Exceptions include the bacon, which is sourced from the South's best artisanal purveyor, Allan Benton, just down the road.

blackberryfarm.com
1471 West Millers Cove Road
+1 865 984 8166
Lunch 12–2.30pm, dinner by reservation only

THE WILLOWS INN
Lummi Island, Washington State, U.S.A.

What we love: For a culinary experience worth going to the ends of the earth for (or at least the ends of the contiguous U.S.), head to this remote, 10-square-mile (26-square-kilometer) island off the coast of Washington, where James Beard Award–winning chef and Noma alum Blaine Wetzel has created a forage-focused fine dining experience. Wetzel, a Washington native, uses only hyper-local ingredients harvested or sourced on the island, resulting in a menu firmly rooted in its terroir. The dishes may sound simple, but they're exquisite in their invariable freshness, meticulous preparation, and striking presentation. Book a cozy room in the main inn or rent one of the spacious guesthouses, several of which are beachfront.

House specialty: The 22-course tasting menu changes seasonally, with highlights including toasted kale leaves, herbed tostada, and spot prawns in rhubarb ceviche.

willows-inn.com
2579 W Shore Drive
+1 888 294 2620

Opposite page: In the vineyard at Vik Chile; this page, top: fresh from the garden; this page, middle: chairs with a view at Blackberry Farm; this page, bottom: cocktails at The Willows Inn

VIK CHILE
Millahue Valley, Chile

What we love: A wine connoisseur's dream, Alex and Carrie Vik's secluded luxury hotel revolves around the 11,000-acre (4452-hectare) vineyard where some of the country's finest wines are being produced. Revel in one of 22 light-filled rooms or in the cantilevered, panoramic pool or in the spa, where treatments incorporate ingredients taken from the terroir. Enlist one of the wonderful huasos (horsemen) for a bespoke tour of the vineyards, attend a barbecue among the vines, and pair house wines with gastronomic treats at the contemporary, art-inflected Milla Milla restaurant. A cast of local characters provides the best-of-the-best raw ingredients – figs, tomatoes, sea salt sourced from the local 400-year-old salt farm Los Cisnes – and tell the full story of the destination.
House specialty: Slow-cooked lamb shanks, Chilean eel, and wild boar served a la plancha in an unfussy family-style setting.

vikchile.com
+569 5668 4853

Fresh seafood on the grill at The Willows Inn

LIFE-CHANGING TIP #05

Our Favorite Food Halls

Here's one trend we can get behind. We love food emporia that offer an overview of the local culinary scene at kiosks and counters, eateries and grocers. Whether high design or low-fi, old school or new, they're worth adding to your list, especially if you're pressed for time. Come hungry and ready to explore through small bites or proper meals – and don't forget the souvenirs.

El Nacional, Barcelona, Spain
elnacionalbcn.com

Grand Central Market,
Los Angeles, California, U.S.A.
grandcentralmarket.com

Market on Main,
Johannesburg, South Africa
marketonmain.co.za

Markthalle Neun,
Berlin, Germany
markthalleneun.de

Foodhallen, Amsterdam,
The Netherlands
foodhallen.nl

St. Roch Market,
New Orleans, Louisiana, U.S.A.
strochmarket.com

Old Airport Road Food Centre,
51 Old Airport Road
Singapore

Smorgasburg,
New York City, New York, U.S.A.
smorgasburg.com

Östermalms Saluhall,
Stockholm, Sweden
ostermalmshallen.se

Isetan, Tokyo, Japan
isetan.mistore.jp

TENKU-NO-MORI
Kyushu, Japan

What we love: Translated as 'Forest in the Sky', this incredibly secluded, money-is-no-object immersive experience includes a mere five villas in a huge expanse of nature – 148 acres (60 hectares) – in a mountain forest on the south-west tip of Japan's Kyushu Island. Each structure on the property has floor-to-ceiling windows, exposed beams, and vast wood decks nestling hot springs and open-air baths, giving way to panoramic views. Guests can enjoy ice-cold champagne while rocking from a tree swing or stroll the ryokan's terraced farm, which produces nearly everything served on site, including some 30 vegetable varieties. Food is not traditionally kaiseki (a traditional multi-course meal showcasing a variety of kitchen skills), but wholly inspired by nature. Served in guest rooms or al fresco, meals are included in the price of the stay. Day-trippers may organize wellness treatments and a gourmet picnic on the grounds and book in at the family's nearby rustic, but no less lovely, lodge, Gajoen.

House specialty: The free-range chicken that the area is known for. It's a delicacy to eat it raw here.

tenkunomori.net
899-6507 Kagoshima Prefecture
+81 995 76 0777

Opposite page, top: Cottage living; opposite page, bottom: the kitchen at La Grenouillère; this page: blossoms in Japan

LA GRENOUILLÈRE
Nord-Pas-de-Calais, France

What we love: A young Alexandre Gauthier took over his family's 1900s-era inn, hired a set designer to give it a theatrical look, and made dining the main act, winning two Michelin stars in the process. Besides the century-old buildings on the premises, two sleek additions made by architect Patrick Bouchain give the property an out-of-the-ordinary aesthetic. The dark and dramatic dining room opens onto wild greenery, and though the plating is meticulously au naturale – like an offering of foraged finds from the woods – expect nothing less than a radical multi-course lunch or dinner of elemental creativity. Everything is sourced (hunted, gathered, grown) locally and used freely and can be paired with nearly 500 expressions of French wine. Breakfast is served in the rooms, a mix of contemporary stylings in a rustic-chic farmhouse or semi-buried cottages around the main building with bay windows overlooking the countryside and gardens, private sitting areas, wood stoves, and soaking tubs. Take an afternoon to stroll through the excellent farmers' market and food shops, and lunch at Gauthier's casual Froggy's Tavern in Montreuil-sur-Mer, just inland from the stylish English Channel resort Le Touquet. The regularly changing menu offers delights on the rotisserie. It's an easy overnight trip from London or Paris (and half the price of many of those cities' best restaurants), promising a little bit of wild country in a weekend's time.
House specialty: Delights from a 25-mile (40-kilometer) radius of the Opal Coast could include langoustines, crab blini, honeycomb, pigeon, tall puffs of brioche, and wild strawberries with chervil.

lagrenouillere.fr
19 Rue de la Grenouillère
+33 3 21 06 07 22
April–June, September–October: lunch Friday–Sunday; dinner Wednesday–Monday
July–August: lunch Wednesday–Sunday; dinner every day
November–March: lunch Friday–Sunday, dinner Thursday–Monday

PART V

Wandering for Wellness

All the Feel-Good Places

Hello. Namaste. Please remove your shoes, have a drink of water, take a deep breath. Now let it out. Good. You have arrived just in time. It's the advent of wellness travel. And it feels really good.

Our current cultural obsession with all things healthy-ish – exercise classes, smoothie bowls, meditation apps, chakra balancing – has been fully embraced by the travel industry in the form of floating gyms, global detox retreats, traveling boot camps, personal training concierges, and hotel running programs, to barely scratch the surface. Traveler demands for paleo meals and acupuncture and three-ounce bottles of sulfate-free shampoo are met with enthusiasm in many surprising destinations all over the world. No one bats an eye at protein smoothies on the room service menu, yoga classes on the hotel rooftop, or astrology readings in the lobby.

At Fathom, we don't think of wellness travel as a one-size-fits-all vacation model – though we do believe that the act of traveling can generally cure whatever ails you. Boutique fitness programs and cutting-edge juice bars are meaningful amenities for the healthy set, but just about

everyone breathes easier waking up to a gorgeous natural landscape after a restful night of sleep.

Wellness travel is sometimes detoxing but rarely punishing, and though it may include swim-up bars serving açai, for us it also includes ancient walking paths, forest bathing rituals, high-energy vortexes, spiritual meccas, and (eventually) higher planes of being.

You could spend a lifetime exploring the world through this lens. Why not start by building a healthy relationship with these iconic destinations?

Opposite page: Surf scene at Hermosa Beach, California; this page: a gentle reminder from the streets of Amsterdam

KYOTO, JAPAN

A few days in Japan's spiritual and cultural heart is the best antidote to the fast and furious pace of modern-day life. It's both an ancient village and an urban city: travelers are just as likely see a businessman zipping by on his bicycle as a group of kimono-clad tourists shuffling down the street – or, if their eyes are peeled, a real geisha.

One of the most majestic aspects of Kyoto is its collection of temples and shrines. There are 2000 in all – each more beautiful than the last – exuding a sense of calm felt with the first step off the high-speed shinkansen (bullet train). Fushimi Inari-taisha, a Shinto shrine at the base of a mountain, is a wonderful place to visit, especially for a meditative early morning hike under its 50,000 orange torii gates, which snake through the woods in colorful trails (inari.jp). With enough planning and the proper permission, travelers may be granted a visit to Zen Buddhist temple Saihō-ji, famed for its stunning moss garden. To enter, visitors must copy a prayer with an ink brush before chanting scripture with Japanese monks.

Tenryū-ji Shigetsu, a tatami-mat restaurant inside Arashiyama's Tenryū-ji Temple, serves sophisticated shojin ryori (vegetarian Buddhist cuisine) in a serene setting (tenryuji.com).

Be warned, it only takes one dip at a local onsen to become a furo-aholic (bathing obsessive).

SANTA FE, NEW MEXICO

The oldest capital in the United States, a village of ancient pueblos and sacred ruins tucked into a valley of the Rio Grande, has been drawing creative types, spiritual seekers, and healers for centuries. Maybe it's the change in altitude. Or the brilliant blue skies set against the majestic red rock landscape. Or the pathway for spiritual exploration. Santa Fe is said to be a spiritual vortex, energetically aligned to attract mystical and healing energies. Travelers from all walks of life partake in the area's alternative healing traditions.

Inspired by Japanese mountain hot spring resorts with traditional gardens and woodwork, Ten Thousand Waves is an East-meets-West spa experience in the tranquil foothills of the mysterious Sangre de Cristo Mountains (tenthousandwaves.com). At Four Seasons Resort Rancho Encantado, guests can sign up for the EQUUS Experience, a unique series of interactions with horses that provides personal insight and wisdom (equussantafe.com).

Thirty miles north of Santa Fe at El Santuario de Chimayó, considered the Lourdes of America, people of all faiths make pilgrimages in search of miracle cures for emotional and physical ailments (holychimayo.us).

Further afield, in Rio Arriba County, the starkly haunting Ghost Ranch, with its sweeping and gorgeous scenes of red rock formations and dramatic, rocky mountain range, is where artist Georgia O'Keeffe spent her summers painting (ghostranch.org). Because no cameras or phones are allowed for photographs, a walk through the place is an exercise in taking in the little details, the larger landscape, and the sensation of light.

osite page:
to temples;
page, top:
thwest
ng scene; this
e, bottom:
ic desert
ls

Sacred Talismans

Create a ritual at home with these sensory souvenirs.

Colorado or California CBD Oil
This one does it all, folks. Reduce pain, quell anxiety, improve your mood, and clear the mind with a vial of pure cannabidiol oil from the hemp plant.

Tibetan Singing Bowl
A standing bell, made from bronze, emits a soothing, high-pitched sound when hit with a wooden mallet, sending vibrations through the body.

Santa Fe Smudge Sticks
A bundle of dried herbs bound with string clears bad juju from a room (and looks nice on a mantle).

Blue Lagoon Silica Mud
Sourced from the bottom of Iceland's famous milky blue pool, the exfoliating and cleansing power of the creamy white mud whips problem skin into shape.

Mysore Sandalwood Oil
A sweet, woody-smelling oil from India helps achieve mental clarity and functions as an antiseptic to treat wounds and blemishes.

Maneki-neko Lucky Cat
Stash one of these Japanese charms — which date back to the Edo period — away for good fortune at home and in business.

LIFE-CHANGING TIP #06

Six Pilgrimages that Could Change Your Life

Whether you're seeking religious answers, reflecting on life, or simply clocking the steps, a lengthy walk in a scenic setting on a time-worn route can be a transformative experience for any modern wayfarer.

KUMANO KODŌ

A series of ancient routes crisscrossing Japan's densely forested Kii Peninsula, these sacred trails south of Osaka have been used by emperors and samurai since the 10th century.

Pit stop: Take a breather at the bright-orange Seiganto-ji temple with the 436-foot-tall (133-meter-tall) Nachi Falls as your backdrop.

INCA TRAIL

Follow the footsteps of one of the world's smartest civilizations by traversing the majestic Andean landscape to get to the ancient Inca city Machu Picchu.

Photo op: Llama photobombing is a real thing here. Be on the lookout for the wonderfully weird-looking creatures — your Instagram followers will repay you with likes. Just watch out for the snacks in your backpack: the llamas aren't shy, and they love a stolen snack.

incatrailperu.com

CAMINO DE SANTIAGO

Pilgrims have traveled the 600-mile (965-kilometer) route through Northern Spain's countryside for more than a millennium. The journey can take nearly a month to complete, depending on your pace.

Road snack: Snack on an anchovy sandwich and cafe con leche at Café Iruña (cafeiruna.com) on the Plaza del Castillo (famous for being Hemingway's hangout during Pamplona's running of the bulls).

santiago-compostela.net

MOUNT KAILASH

Considered by Buddhists and Hindus to be one of the most sacred places on the planet, the trek around the holiest peak in Tibet is one of the most dangerous and challenging pilgrimages in the world.

Divine ritual: Total enlightenment is closer than you think. It's said that 108 circumambulations of the mountain base is all it takes.

THE ST. OLAV WAYS

Behold Norway's magnificent expressions of nature — blue fjords, fog-cloaked valleys, moose — before paying your respects at the grave of King Olav at Trondheim's Nidaros Cathedral.

Extra credit: Power through an extra 172 steps to the top of the gothic tower for the best views of the city.

pilegrimsleden.no

VIA FRANCIGENA

Pilgrims take the ancient road connecting Canterbury to Rome, stop at the tomb of Peter the Apostle and maybe carbo-load on pasta.

Proof of purchase: A special passport is available to pilgrims interested in gathering stamps along the route. Once in Rome, request a certificate of pilgrimage called a testimonium.

viefrancigene.org

BALI, INDONESIA

This magical Indonesian island, often referred to as the last paradise on Earth, has become a refuge for the surfers, partiers, bohemians, and digital nomads of the world. Surrounded by the Indian Ocean and the Java Sea, this idyllic tropical province is known for its white sandy beaches, lush and terraced rice fields, and rugged coastlines. Anchored by a slower pace of life and deep spiritual practice, Balinese Hinduism permeates every aspect of the island – from the thousands of temples to the many cultural celebrations.

Seekers who appreciate a midcentury design nod in the middle of the jungle should stay at Katamama Hotel, a boutique hideaway with lots of authentic local touches (katamama.com). The hotel was designed by an Indonesian architect using hand-pressed bricks produced in the same vein as the island's temples.

Those looking for a restorative detox will find it at Sukhavati Ayurvedic Retreat, which uses the 5000-year-old system of natural healing to reset the mind, body, and soul (sukhavatibali.com).

For a freeing weekend escape, the small island of Nusa Lembongan has potholed trails through scrubby forests, chickens running wild, blue waters, little bays, surf spots, and lots of natural beauty.

KERALA, INDIA

Kerala ticks just about every soothing box: tropical beaches, jungles filled with exotic wildlife, and yogis perfecting their practice at the local ashrams. Often referred to as India-lite because of its appeal to Westerners, this energetic state located at the country's southernmost tip attracts all types of travelers.

This is the ground zero of Ayurveda so try to schedule a relaxing treatment with charismatic Dr. P. Sambhu, a well-known third-generation physician who has been practicing for nearly two decades in India, Europe, and the Americas and now works at the Ayushya center (ayushya.com). Then treat yourself to sadhya, the traditional local vegetarian feast served on a plantain leaf with boiled rice and host of side dishes.

A canoe cruise through the canals of the backwaters, particularly in Alappuzha, where people are going about their daily lives – bathing, washing clothes, and just spending time with family and friends along the rocky ledges – may just change your perspective on life.

This page, top: Bali motorcycle ride; this page, bottom: a rainbow of spices; overleaf page: iconic prayer flags in Tibet

TIBETAN PLATEAU

The hidden jewel of the East has called out to mystics, monks, clerics, refugees, and believers for centuries. The Tibetan Plateau, or The Roof of the World, is a unique elevated stretch of land covering most of Tibet, parts of western China, and India. It is nearly 14,800 feet (4510 meters) in elevation and is surrounded by massive mountain ranges, including the world's two highest summits, Mount Everest and K2. Shamanistic, tantric, and Buddhist influences collide on this sacred parcel, which is said to have 'power places' saturating the surrounding water, plants, stones, and earth with fields of energy.

Twenty minutes outside the famous Tibetan monastic town of Labrang, China, on the plateau are a handful of stylish log cabins and handwoven yak-hair tents that comprise Norden Camp (nordentravel.com). The setting is lush. The retreats and immersions vary: yoga, chakra healing, textile making, high-altitude mind and body training. The landscape and location are remarkable: a day that begins with sunshine can end with snowfall. (The area is a traditional winter grazing ground for nomadic herds.) Whole families are encouraged to book their stay – The Tibet Autonomous Region (T.A.R) is a land of compassion and kindness, perfect for children.

Getting Into Hot Water

Mother Nature's baths are a beautiful thing.

EVASON MA'IN HOT SPRINGS
Madaba, Jordan

It's a scenic hour-long drive from Amman's Queen Alia International Airport to this resort and spa nestled in a spectacular mountain landscape surrounded by palm trees, hot spring waterfalls, and natural saltwater pools loaded with therapeutic properties. Treatments focus on the mineral-rich waters and sea salt therapies. Be sure to visit the cave sauna, maybe before a Bedouin feast on the hot springs terrace. Excursions to the Dead Sea, which is 20 minutes away, are a must. The proximity of the hotel to some of the most important religious sites in the world – the Tomb of Moses, the baptism site of Jesus – gives the place an unmistakable weightiness despite all the floating on water.

Sowayma, 17173, Ma'In
+1 866 599 6674

THE ESALEN INSTITUTE
Big Sur, California, U.S.A.

This famed hippie compound on a wild stretch of California coastline operates as a non-profit retreat center and intentional community – a happenin' spot since the '60s, when Hunter S. Thompson roamed the wooded grounds, Joan Baez worked in the quinoa-and-kale-loving cafeteria, and, in the realm of fiction, *Mad Men* protagonist Don Draper found everlasting inner peace and a gazillion-dollar ad idea. The sprawling grounds have simple accommodations, yurts for meditation, and sitting areas for self-reflection. But it's most famous for its rustic outdoor baths open 24/7 for guests (and from 1–3am for visitors) perched on a cliff over the Pacific Ocean. The local Esselen tribe used the baths for 6000 years, and it was probably swimsuit-optional then, too.

esalen.org
55000 Highway 1
U.S.A.: 1 888 837 2536;
International: +1 703 342 0500

Opposite page: Strolling along the beach; this page, top: floating in the Dead Sea; this page, bottom: the coastline from Esalen Institute, Big Sur

7132 THERME
Vals, Switzerland

You'll need to have your wits about you for the drive from
Zurich – which involves barreling through mountain tunnels
and hugging roads as they swerve around sheep outposts and
thin streams of water diving off grassy cliffs. Eventually you'll
approach the town of Vals, with its fudge stripes and wooden
shutters carved with hearts. A few more turns, and you'll
end up at the base of a retro-futuristic hotel cradled in an
ancient valley of the Alps. The spa, which accesses the town's
pristine natural spring, lives below the seventh-floor lobby.
Minimalist architect Peter Zumthor designed it as a modern
temple to water rituals. After a day on the slopes, silent bathers
spend evenings moving from outdoor pool to indoor plunge to
aromatherapy bath (filled with delicate flower petals) to sound
grotto to a drinking stone, and back again.

7132.com
+41 58 713 20 00
Wednesday–Sunday 11am–8pm

RETREAT SPA AT BLUE LAGOON
Grindavík, Iceland

Just about anyone who passes through Iceland takes a dip in
the famed geothermal spa located conveniently close to the
airport, which has given it an unfortunate reputation as a
tourist trap. But the Retreat at Blue Lagoon, the first hotel and
day spa of its kind in Iceland, has created a bathing experience
that recaptures the serenity and isolation the landmark has
lost. Day visitors and overnight guests can access the main
lagoon, of course, but they are also privy to a private and
secluded spa flowing from the same geothermal wellspring.
Volcanic earth meets Nordic air and a bevy of water treatments,
scrubbing rituals, and unadulterated panoramas.

bluelagoon.com
Norðurljósavegur 11, 240 Grindavík
+354 420 8800

Ground yourself among the majestic
California redwoods

NEGOMBO
Ischia, Italy

People have been flocking to Ischia, the island off the coast of Naples that's not Capri, for its healing waters and mineral-rich volcanic mud since 700 BC. One of the better ways to experience them is at Negombo, a seaside complex of beach, gardens, and hydrothermal experiences – hot tubs, Kneipp baths, waterfalls, saunas, and steam rooms. Pay the entrance fee and spend the day splashing about with abandon. The water park (that's what they call it) is built onto a hillside and consists of a maze of pools, caves, grottoes, hydro-massages, and other creative aquatic creations and art installations. Pause for breaks in the hammocks and on sun beds, and revive yourself with fresh juices at the cafe. The beach is a private cove lined with lounge chairs and umbrellas. It can get crowded, but it's big enough that it's never obnoxious. A spa offers a variety of treatments, but the showstopper is the scorching hammam, where lithe Italians perched on a giant marble slab baste themselves with cooling water as sunlight streams from pinholes in the ceiling.

negombo.it
Baia di San Montano, 80076 Lacco Ameno
+39 081 986152
8.30am–7pm

FOREST BATHING
Various locations

Those averse to getting wet may appreciate the Japanese practice of shinrin-yoku, or 'taking in the forest atmosphere', something humans can do in any wooded environment. No water necessary. The premise is simple: Go deep under a canopy of trees, take in the sights and sounds and smells, connect with the forest floor by removing your shoes and walking around barefoot (it's called 'earthing'), and absorb all the physical and psychological benefits. It's not hiking; it's more like meandering. Studies have shown that regular excursions to the forest reduce anxiety, lower blood pressure, quell anger, improve sleep, strengthen the immune system, accelerate recovery, and even deepen relationships. A guide can make the experience richer by helping to open your senses, hone your intuition, and guide you through local flora and fauna. In addition to Japan (whose cypress forests in the Kiso region of Gifu Prefecture are deemed particularly beautiful), our short list includes Denmark (the green woodlands on top of the chalky cliffs of Møns Klint), Germany (the dense evergreens of the Black Forest), and the Pacific Northwest of the U.S. (the stately Redwood National and State parks are home to the tallest trees on Earth).

PART VI

Digital Nomads

Take Your
Show on the Road

For many, figuring out how to avoid the ho-hum office lifestyle is akin to figuring out life. We are no longer living in the era of the Company Man. We live in the gig economy, and it has its pros and cons.

We want our careers to feel meaningful, which might mean forfeiting job stability, and we want to ensure we have a good work–life balance, which is anathema to the capitalist notion that more work is always better. This disruption in job standards – commuting to an office, working from nine to five – is challenging the way we think about work, down to the most fundamental question of *where* we work. If your professional life consists of projects, gigs, or hustles that are not location-specific, does it matter where you are doing it, as long as you get it done? Probably not.

Which then leads to the possibility of doing what you do remotely in a different – and more exciting! – setting. Like a beach in Bali, or a coffee shop in Paris, or a cozy ship cabin charging across the Atlantic. Imagine earning your living while soaking up new cultures, sights, foods, and experiences. It's the ultimate modern travel fantasy: becoming a digital nomad.

Since the debut of the travel memoir, writers have documented the thrills of waking up in a new place and settling in at a cafe table, or ambling for hours, stimulated by the inspiration that comes from watching life unfold on the streets or connecting with like-minded wanderers. In more recent times, new developments – like a technology-driven permalance economy, home-share platforms, free global telecom services, co-working spaces, and social media – have made becoming a digital nomad ever more enticing and doable. Today's roaming employee can work hard, play hard, and travel hard – and then do it all again in an exciting new setting the next time they catch that travel bug. A digital nomad lives everywhere and nowhere at the same time.

For those who aren't confined to a cubicle – writers, designers, developers, creators, consultants, photographers, or any mobile professional – and who have the appetite for

adventure, taking a leap outside the office seems like a fun and fulfilling way to live a freelance life. The reality, however, has its challenges. Picture yourself turning up in a strange town – you might have landed in the middle of the night and you're probably alone – and figuring out how to set up shop for a few months. Where will you find reliable wifi? Which neighborhood fits you best? Where's the grocery store? And, wow, could you use a cup of good coffee.

As daunting as it sounds, more and more people are not only making it work but are thriving in this lifestyle. Not surprisingly, many are documenting their adventures and best practices. It seems a good rule of thumb is to allocate at least three months to any one place. This keeps the client roster, bank account, and sanity intact. By sharing what they've learned along the way, the trailblazing digital nomads are helping and inspiring others who want to follow in their footsteps and trade complacent routines for the scary thrill of the unknown – and reap the incredible rewards of deep friendships, newfound knowledge, and a greater understanding of the world.

Every corner of the globe is available for exploration. So how does a deliberate roamer decide where to go? Some places are hubs of activity and opportunity; others are laidback, allowing for slow, thoughtful work weeks. We suggest the destinations listed below for their essential qualities: great community, reliable wifi, and affordable daily living. Consider these starting points for your future adventures as a digital nomad.

Opposite page:
Co-working in Bali;
overleaf page: Chiang
Mai, Thailand

LIFE-CHANGING TIP #07

Will Work for Travel (and Vice Versa)

When it comes to balancing work and travel, these Fathom contributors make the living look easy. Add them to your Instagram for a steady stream of wanderlust.

Alpana Deshmukh
@alpana.deshmukh

Anna Petrow
@annapetrow

Chris Schalkx
@chrisschalkx

Daniel Schwartz
@hellowithyou

Dulci Edge
@ladulcivida

Emily Nathan
@ernathan

Erica Firpo
@ericafirpo

Jessica Cantlin
@feed.
my.wanderlust

Kasia Dietz
@kasiadietz

Kate Donnelly
@k8bdonnelly

Katie McKnoulty
@thetravellinglight

Larkin Clark
@larkinclark

Lee Litumbe
@spiritedpursuit

Lucy Laucht
@lucylaucht

Mark Gray
@daysofmrgray

Michaela Trimble
@michaelatrimble

Paul Jebara
@pawljebara

Pauline Egge
@petitepassport

Tanveer Badal
@tanveerbadal

Victoria Cairo
@victoria.a.cairo

THE STANDARD BEARER: CHIANG MAI, THAILAND

Thailand's most connected city tops every digital nomad's list for a reason.

Ask any seasoned digital nomad about their favorite remote working experience and chances are they'll go on about Chiang Mai. Long a hideaway for the expat community, Thailand's second city has become a central hub for remote workers from around the world. It's not uncommon to stumble across a co-working space on a walk through town or sit next to and strike up conversation with a fellow nomad at a random coffee shop. It's this strong sense of community, of being in the same boat with a bunch of like-minded, motivated professionals, that continues to draw former nine-to-fivers who want a comfortable launching pad for their brave new lives.

The low average cost of living also helps. A monthly budget of 33,000 Thai baht ($1000USD) goes a long way when room and board is abundant and affordable, eating out is cheaper than cooking at home (and arguably more delicious), quality coffee from the countryside costs a quick dollar, tuk-tuk rides clock in at a few bucks, and free high-speed wifi is easy to find, especially with a local phone plan that opens up a ton of hotspots. Co-working spaces, which tend to have the fastest internet, are widespread and offer sweet deals, but it's the atmosphere of collaboration they foster that make them a priceless fixture in Chiang Mai's professional scene.

Though the city has adapted in recent years to meet the needs of its growing tourist and expat populations, its personality remains intact. There are temples and bustling markets everywhere, a youthful energy in the air thanks to the city's three universities, and ample day trip opportunities to sample the north's natural beauty. Chiang Mai is one of the more laidback hubs in Southeast Asia, a big plus for those who can only handle so much hustle and bustle.

Alternative cities: Ho Chi Minh City, Vietnam

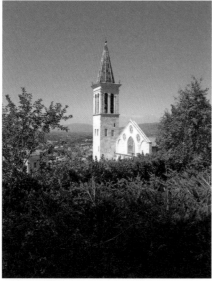

THE VILLAGE FANTASY:
SPOLETO, UMBRIA, ITALY

Where life is as slow and steady as freshly laundered clothes drying in the sun. Quiet time plus small town charm equals clarity in work and commitment to the good life.

The summer of Fathom's third birthday, we took up a friend's offer to stay at his family's Italian palazzo in Spoleto, a sleepy Umbrian town at the foothills of the Apennines. The home had been uninhabited for a few years and was notable for its grand frescoes, velvet furnishings, and remarkably reliable wifi connection. Our friend wanted to breathe life into the house; we wanted relief from the startup grind. Of course, it's not every day that an invitation arrives to move your office headquarters from a cramped co-working space in downtown Manhattan to an inspiringly romantic old European home in a tiny medieval village – and to do it free of charge – but one of the morals of this story is that some opportunities are too good to pass up.

Another moral of this story is that travelers who choose small towns over big cities are forced to act like locals – which is a good thing. In Spoleto, instead of rushing around like the wound-up New Yorkers we usually are, we kept things mellow, giving way to nonnas trekking up cobblestone streets, throwing open the shutters to watch passersby, taking evening passeggiate (the Italian ritual of strolling at night) through the piazzas, and ending the night not with obsessive Instagram scrolling but with local wine, espresso, and poker by candlelight.

Living in a village made us feel responsible for learning about its history, its cultural offerings, quirks, local players, and lasting pasta traditions (including strangozzi, an Umbrian variation of fat linguini served with fava beans, pancetta, and pecorino). It gave us the time and space to think and talk in-depth about Fathom, and what we hoped it would become. A sleepy town is a great home base for those looking to hash out the details for a new project or business, immerse themselves in a new language, or hit a deadline with little distraction. Ask friends and family for introductions to their friends and family in little-known neighborhoods as a means to figuring out if this is the kind of short-term lifestyle for you.

Alternative villages: Hydra, Greece; Guanajuato, Mexico; Šibenik, Croatia

THE TECH UPSTART: TALLINN, ESTONIA

The birthplace of Skype is making it easier to start something great.

Tallinn has a game plan: to become the next great place to launch a tech unicorn. Estonia's government is debuting a nomad visa, the first of its kind in the world, which will allow 'location-independent' workers to be in the country legally for up to 12 months at a time – quadruple the usual three-month visa. This means not having to fly under the radar jockeying short-term tourist visas like most digital nomads do. This is a boon for teams looking for enough stability to get things off the ground or work on long-term projects while benefiting from all that Tallinn and Estonia at large have to offer, which is to say: the world's second fastest public wifi; plenty of parks, cute cafes, and co-working spaces; a vibrant summer culture; and a tapped-in startup community teeming with cool creatives, entrepreneurs, and IT whizzes, the likes of which helped launch Skype almost two decades ago. It's an exciting city to start a business in, and an easy one at that, as the country's advanced digital infrastructure makes it possible to launch a startup in less time than it takes to finish a latte.

The only downside? Winters are rough. But on the new nomad visa, residents get 90 days of travel to countries within the Schengen Area (a zone of 26 European nations allowing unrestricted movement between borders), making it incredibly easy to take a quick trip to Italy, Greece, or Spain to catch some rays and recharge.

Alternative cities: Tel Aviv, Israel; Dublin, Ireland

Opposite page, top: Author Jeralyn Gerba at work; opposite page, bottom: the cathedral in Spoleto, Italy; this page, top: outisde Telliskivi Creative City in Tallinn, Estonia; this page, bottom: scenes from inside Telliskivi Creative City; overleaf page: work meets play in Bali

THE ISLAND OF WORK–LIFE BALANCE: BALI, INDONESIA

Low-key, lush, and inexpensive, you can live well and experience the power of nature at your doorstep.

A few years ago, we started noticing that many of our contributors were headed to Ubud, Bali. One of them, Katie McKnoulty, who documents her travels on her blog, The Traveling Light, wrote about her experience making the world her home, observing that Ubud is a leafy green refuge for people fresh out of a break-up or the nine-to-five. People come humble and hungry to start anew. It's a likely meeting spot for the spiritual set, the mind-body connectors, and the perennial wanderers, a place where people go to worship wellness, meditate, and operate on new plains.

As if the island's spectacular beaches, lush jungles, aquamarine waters, healthy foods, and wildly cheap massages weren't welcoming enough, the local community continually opens its arms to waves of newcomers. One thing that struck a chord with McKnoulty was the way strangers struck up interesting conversations at every turn. 'People say things like, "I've just really gotten into my ecstatic dance since I've been here," and "If I can just get this accelerator funding for my app, I know things will really take off for me"'. Life here never feels regular or boring. Beware though: life is so easy in Ubud that many people don't ever want to leave. Transitioning back to the real world can be tough.

Alternative cities: Colombo, Sri Lanka; Canggu, Bali

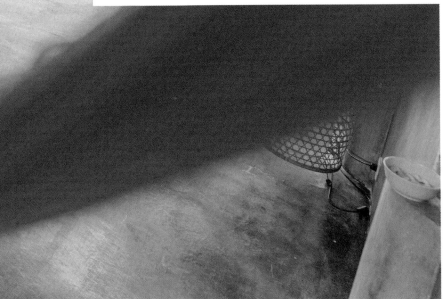

THE CHANNEL-YOUR-ARTIST CITY:
BERLIN, GERMANY

Artists, creatives, and late-night revelers flock to the progressive, well-connected city for its German efficiency and anything-goes vibe.

For a short stint right before the launch of Fathom, Berlin was one of our hunting grounds for inspiration – a city operating 24/7, with enough museums and cultural institutions to balance out all of the debaucherous nightclubs and underground party places. (We made sure we had a healthy diet of both.) By day, the place seemed to be run by artists, musicians, writers, and freelancers with Big Ideas. Entrepreneurs on the make had the flexibility to live well – that is to say affordably and productively, and with a healthy work–life balance. Berlin is a place where office workers break together for a hot meal (instead of eating sad deli salads in front of their computer), where suits and academics have a passion for record collecting and throw gender non-binary leather parties. There's an edgy quality to the people and the place. Nothing is too clean, too bourgeois, or too uptight, and it's an easy hub for those who need or want easy access to the rest of Europe. In summer, its cafe culture, green space, and open container laws make for a general sense of camaraderie – more so than most international cities – which contributes to the overall feeling that we're all in this together.

Alternative cities: Prague, Czech Republic; Budapest, Hungary; Lisbon, Portugal

FUN FACT: American astronaut Peggy Whitson takes her work to new heights and extremes – literally! – shattering records as she goes. Among her achievements: she's the oldest female astronaut to fly in space, has completed the most spacewalks by a woman, and has spent the most time on spacewalks.

THE DIAMOND IN THE ROUGH: MEDELLÍN, COLOMBIA

Big-city bustle, warm hospitality, and great weather make for a healthy work environment in an under-the-radar locale.

Forget *Narcos*. Medellín has reinvented itself. A ton of urban development and a burgeoning creative class have made Medellín the city of choice in South America for digital nomads. It's a big place with a lot going on – cool hotels, restaurants, cafes, and co-working spaces for work and socializing. And it's not the kind of place that sucks newcomers in and spits them back out.

Medellín has a warmth that many major cities lack. Locals, who refer to themselves as Paisas, are incredibly welcoming and have no problem pointing people in the right direction – to the market, the best lunch spot, or the best bar. Basic Spanish is useful in many situations, but rusty grammar won't drag on one's social life. Most friends are made on the dance floor.

The city, though, is not without its problems. Traffic is tough, local jobs don't pay much, and there are still neighborhoods best avoided at night. But nothing takes away from what a sweet deal the city is for digital nomads. It's a relatively sane flight from most major American cities and shares a familiar time zone, making it easy to work with clients in the U.S. Housing is affordable and so is eating out – a big plate of rice, beans, veggies, and protein (known as menú del dia) costs about 12,000 Colombian pesos ($4USD). Getting around is a breeze, whether it's in a cheap Uber or on the metro system, the only one of its kind in Colombia.

The best part: It's roughly 72° F (22°C) year-round. This is perfect weather for meeting both work and fitness goals. A healthy smattering of public outdoor gyms and sidewalk cafes helps the cause.

Alternative cities: Cape Town, South Africa; Oaxaca, Mexico

Opposite page: A plant-filled cafe in Berlin; this page, top: colors of Medellín

The Coolest Co-working Spaces

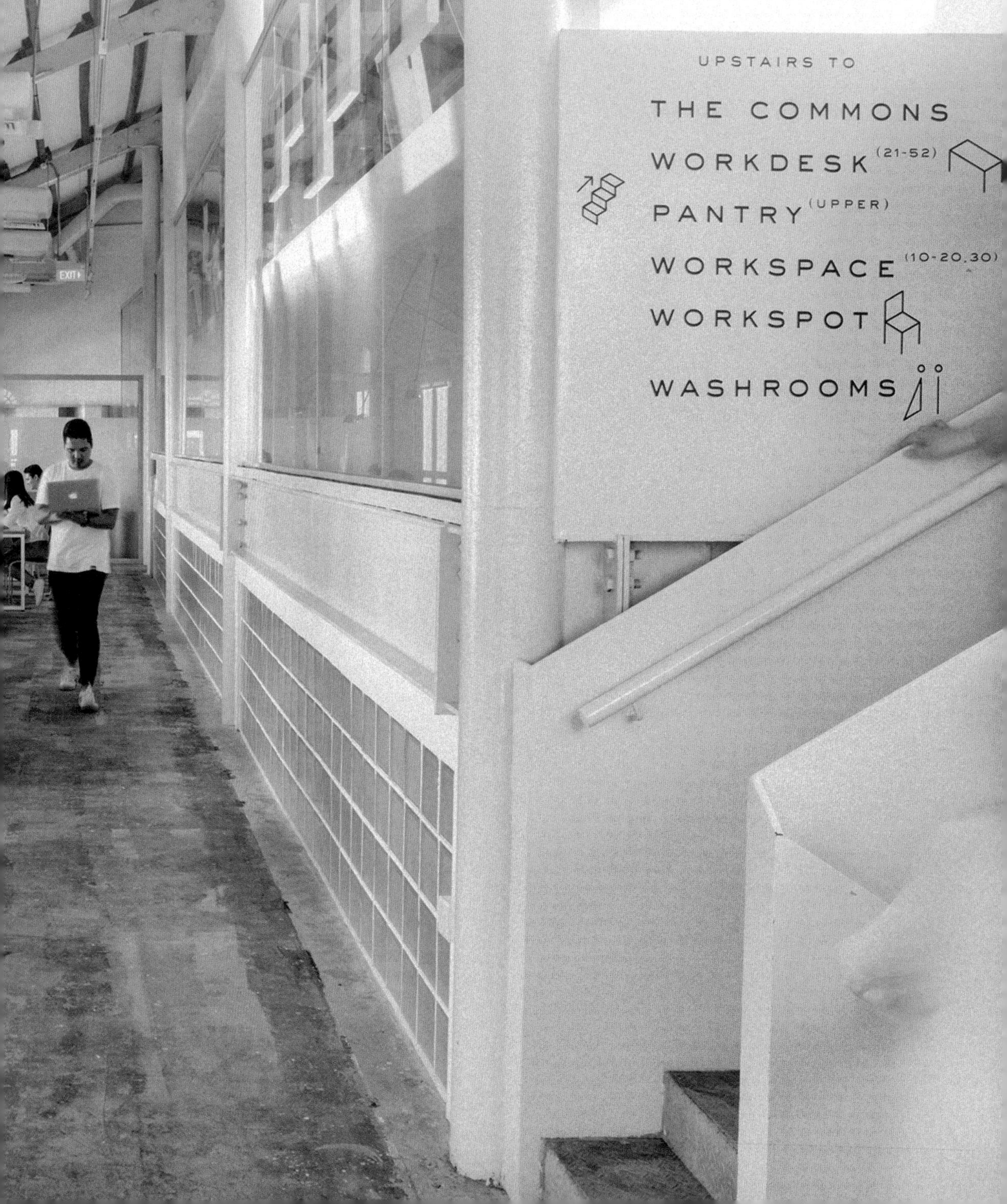
UPSTAIRS TO
THE COMMONS
WORKDESK (21-52)
PANTRY (UPPER)
WORKSPACE (10-20,30)
WORKSPOT
WASHROOMS
EXIT

Taking work on the road to a far-flung destination sounds like the ultimate travel fantasy. Putting up with crowded cafes, shoddy internet connections, and feelings of isolation ... not so much. These beautifully designed co-working spaces are the friendly and welcoming places to be.

SINGAPORE: THE WORKING CAPITOL

The original location, which spans five light-filled, historic shophouses on Keong Saik Road, has multiple event spaces for up to 200 people, a beer garden for after-work socializing, and three restaurants. The second outpost in the CBD has a cafe, bar, restaurant, sky garden, and lap pool.

theworkingcapitol.com
1 Keong Saik Road
+65 6805 4050
Monday–Friday 8.30am–6pm

UBUD, BALI: HUBUD

The all-bamboo co-working space is famous for its friendly community of plugged-in nomads. An all-natural cafe, a rotating series of social and cultural events, and a co-living program geared toward teams looking to get settled quickly make it easy to make friends and feel part of something bigger.

hubud.org
Monkey Forest Road 88x
+62 361 978073

MUMBAI, INDIA: MINISTRY OF NEW

This high-design warehouse helmed by two Dutch nationals has an expansive, open-plan workspace filled with plants, an indoor–outdoor courtyard bathed in natural light, a charming library that doubles as a meeting space, and an artsy cafe serving pastas, salads, and sandwiches.

ministryofnew.in
Kitab Mahal, 3rd Floor, 192 Dadabhai Naoroji Road, Azad Maidan, Fort
Monday–Friday: 9am–9pm, Saturday: 10am–4pm
+91 22 6635 6505

Opposite page: The Working Capitol; this page, top: Relaxing while working at Hubud; this page, bottom: Ministry of New

LATIN AMERICA: SELINA HOTELS

This fast-growing hotel chain is making the digital nomad lifestyle more accessible by pairing co-working space with affordable lodging in city and seaside destinations throughout Central and South America, like Costa Rica, Panama, and Colombia. Membership to all locations makes it possible for workaholics to stage their own re-enactment of *The Motorcycle Diaries* while on deadline.

selina.com

TOKYO, JAPAN: NINETYTWO13

What's not to love about this industrial workshop–inspired office space? It's decked out with reclaimed furniture from around the world and attracts a hip international following. Its spaces include a gourmet kitchen, yoga studio, gym, meeting rooms, workshop, atelier, laundry, and even apartments for rent upstairs. And, should you need reminding, it's in the middle of freaking Tokyo.

tokyochapter.com
Akasaka 9-2-13 minato-ku
+81 03 6721 0175

MONTREAL, CANADA: CREW COLLECTIVE

In a breathtaking former bank building – high ceilings, marble, and bronze galore – the city's creatives gather in private offices, shared workspaces, a full-service cafe, kitchen, lounges, meeting rooms, and a speakeasy.

crewcollectivecafe.com
360 St-Jacques

Opposite page: Getting down to business at Crew Collective; this page, top: a Tokyo rooftop at NinetyTwo13; this page, bottom: another beautiful space by Crew Collective

Hubud co-working space in Bali

LIFE-CHANGING TIP #08

Travel Heroes

Long before the digital nomad meme gained traction, intrepid spirits have explored and shared new horizons of the human experience. In the last 100 years alone, there have been some truly remarkable individuals who have shown us what it looks like when one travels well, lives better, and documents it for the rest of us to see, read, and be inspired by. It's worth taking the time to get to know these OG working travelers.

Zora Neale Hurston

A Harlem Renaissance figure, powerhouse author, and anthropologist, Zora Neale Hurston conducted ethnographic fieldwork with a daredevil streak. She relayed stories of train-jumping and voodoo-researching, wrote about Caribbean folklore, and penned a Florida guidebook in 1939 – traveling the whole time in the face of Jim Crow laws. Pick up a copy of her bold and funny autobiography, *Dust Tracks on a Road*.

Beryl Markham

The badass British-born Kenyan aviator and adventurer claims many firsts: Africa's first thoroughbred racehorse trainer, Africa's first bush pilot, and the first woman to fly solo across the Atlantic from east to west. Her memoir *West with the Night* tells the tales.

Jane Goodall

The renowned octogenarian primatologist spends most of her time on the road (around 300 days annually) speaking up for animals, the environment, and conservation. The story of how she got to this place – sailing to Kenya, meeting an anthropologist, moving into the wilderness to study chimpanzees (accompanied by her London-born mother!), sharing her finds, working tirelessly to establish an institute – is nothing short of inspiring. Catch her on the speaking circuit if you can. And brush up on *In the Shadow of Man*.

Bill Bryson

Prolific, investigative, and generously descriptive, the journalist and memoirist has a knack for capturing small-town, bygone America, Australia, and Britain, among other places, with humor, wit, and grace. Start with a copy of *A Walk in the Woods*.

James Baldwin

Many a would-be writer chased the coattails of the lauded novelist and social critic who lived and wrote freely in Paris in the mid 20th century after escaping overt American racism and homophobia. He arrived on a one-way ticket when he was 24, broke, and with no knowledge of the language. But he made a name for himself and carved out a romantic Parisian intellectual lifestyle, which he chronicled in his 1961 *Esquire* essay, 'The New Lost Generation.'

Andrew Zimmern

It's a joy watching this culinary expert and TV personality voraciously eat his way across the globe, imparting cultural, historical, and culinary knowledge like gifts to viewers. Catch up on reruns of *Bizarre Foods*.

Bruce Chatwin

The bewitching storyteller and English shapeshifter wandered from South America to Australia, trying to understand and reveal the human condition in both his fiction and so-called non-fiction. Take a leap with his groundbreaking travelogue, *In Patagonia*.

Mae Jemison

Art meets science meets humanity for the multi-hyphenate Jemison, an engineer, physician, dancer, NASA astronaut, and first African-American woman to travel to space. Whip-smart, creative, determined, and imaginative, she stretches the limits of possibility at every turn (human interstellar space travel, anyone?). Dig up her Discovery Channel science series, *World of Wonders*, and her memoir for children, *Find Where the Wind Goes*.

Ernest Hemingway

There is probably no better known literary figure and traveling titan of the 20th century. (No matter where we go, it seems Hemingway already had a drink there.) Yes, machismo and bitterness are rife in the famous works of the larger-than-life raconteur, but so is an incredible sense of adventure and longing and mystery that manages to reel us in. Keep up with the action in *The Sun Also Rises*.

Maya Angelou

Known as a monumental figure in poetry and activism, the queen of quotations lived many lives, including that of a singer, dancer, actor, and journalist in Egypt and Ghana. Central themes to her work include identity, journey, and searching for home. Read her lyrical explorations of Africa and the diaspora in *All God's Children Need Traveling Shoes*.

Ernest Shackleton

Unwavering leadership and the fierce will to survive are the lasting impressions the polar explorer made on the world. His failed expedition to the South Pole in the early 1900s persists as a model for crisis management today (ask any MBA student about it). The story is unbelievable and incredibly moving. Read about the legendary – and harrowing – Antarctic expedition in *The Endurance* by Caroline Alexander.

Amelia Earhart

She saw aviation as a chance to bring the world together and encouraged other women to join the ranks as a means of working for peace. Besides being the first woman to cross the Atlantic by air, the passionate pilot volunteered as a nurse's aid for the Red Cross during World War I, counseled students in Purdue's Department of Aeronautics, launched a flight-inspired fashion line, and served as the aviation editor of *Cosmopolitan*, profiling pioneering women. Breeze through her autobiography, *The Fun of It*.

Paul Theroux

This contemporary travel writer has chronicled so many countries, it's overwhelming to see them all in print. What he is most lauded for is his ability to find the truth of a place, often by questioning authority, traveling spontaneously, and getting to know the locals. (As a consequence, from time to time, his books are banned by various governments.) Be transported by his classic travelogue, *The Great Railway Bazaar*.

Anthony Bourdain

With rock-and-roll looks and habits and a take-no-prisoners attitude, the celebrity travel documentarian and chef uncovered the corners of the world in all their gritty realness and down-home deliciousness. Binge-watch episodes of his travel shows, *No Reservations* and *Parts Unknown*.

Pico Iyer

A travel writer who reports on the crossing of cultures is living the experiment: he was born in Britain to Indian parents, lived in California, befriended the 14th Dalai Lama, and resides in Japan with his Japanese wife. Besides crafting beautiful prose about spirituality and finding home, Iyer also tackles the airport, jet lag, displacement, standing still, and the in-between moments of travel. Stream his Ted talks: 'Where Is Home?' and 'The Beauty of What We'll Never Know.'

Rebecca Solnit

The enchanting American essayist and editor has, in her various works, made a case for taking subversive detours of the mind, journeying instead of arriving, and walking to unlock politics, people, and place. She has worked on human rights campaigns, reported on disasters, shared untold histories, and documented the cultural landscape. (Fun fact: the word 'mansplaining' was inspired by one of her essays.) Read her series of autobiographical essays, *A Field Guide to Getting Lost*.

PART VII

Be Good in the World

The World Is What You Make It

We're living in strange and turbulent times, when old political orders are being disrupted and entire peoples are being displaced. And the inevitable result is a strange and turbulent world.

If the mid-20th century was defined by movements and uprisings motivated by democratic and humanitarian hopes and ambitions, the 21st century is establishing itself as an era of instability and insecurity, of terror attacks and tragedies. Civil wars and unrest are leading to massive shifts in migration, as desperate people flee their homes for foreign lands in search of safety and stability, only to find the welcome mat pulled away at increasingly closed borders – even those of solidly democratic countries.

It's easy to think that we're sliding away from progress, and that maybe the only answer in an unstable world is to just stay home.

And yet.

There's another side to this story. It's one of hope. It's one of love. It's the side that says that darkness can't reign forever. That the sun will always rise. That tragedies usually lead to togetherness. That the human spirit will always triumph. That people are fundamentally good.

This is what we focus on when we travel. We embrace our global citizenship – and do our best to ensure that we're always moving through the world with decency, kindness, and warmth.

The world is getting smaller, aided by technology and the immediate dissemination of information. We see the same movies and listen to the same songs. We play Words with Friends and follow the Instagram stories of strangers we stumble upon from Senegal to San Diego. Yet, although we're living in a more connected world, nationalism is on the rise, and along with it xenophobia, racism, and fear. And that's awfully dispiriting.

But it's not hopeless, because the small steps we can take as individuals will have an impact. The cure for xenophobia? Spend time with foreigners. There's no more effective way to realize that we're all pretty much the same. We love to be with our friends. We want to get along with our families. We want to be proud of our work. We like good meals. We celebrate our milestones. We want to have fun. You can change the menu, the music, the setting, the clothes, and the language, but strip that all away, and the essence remains the same.

Realize this, and you'll have an open mind.

Have an open mind, and you'll have an open heart.

If you take this thinking to the next level, you might find yourself not only incorporating humanitarian work into your travels, but rather building your entire journeys around lending a hand. Voluntourism is on the rise, and there are more

Opposite page: Tian Tan Buddha, Hong Kong; this page: a recipe for gratitude

111

opportunities than ever for travelers to give back to the places they visit – and maybe leave them a little bit better than they found them.

In other words, why would you be a spectator when you can be a participant?

And if you're going to be a participant, why not make a proper commitment to it?

Stephanie March, actress, humanitarian, world traveler, and Fathom contributor, long ago decided that she would incorporate what she calls the Humanity Tithe into all her travels. In an essay she wrote for us, she challenges us to do the same:

As I have broadened the scope of my adventures, I have been exposed to more of the grittier realities of life in third-world countries. That stark contrast between those who have so much and those who have nothing is never more apparent than when you open your purse to buy water and realize your purse - your beautiful, stupid purse - cost more than the person selling you the water will see in a year. It's one of the most disorienting, disappointing, and heartbreaking aspects of travel.

It is extremely easy to avoid all such unpleasantness. You can a. never leave the United States or b. swaddle your travel in first-class arrangements, taking great care to avoid seeing the "bad stuff." At least those are the most popular options.

There is, however, a third path, a middle way, that allows the eager visitor the opportunity to celebrate and contribute. I call it the Humanity Tithe.

Here's a good example. On a trip to Cambodia for Christmas, we traveled to Angkor Wat and spent a magical day tromping around the ruins. A glorious tuk-tuk ride through the jungle, a dip in the jade green pool at La Résidence d'Angkor, and two bottles of rosé later, we determined it to be the perfect day.

Cambodia, in addition to being home to magnificent architectural ruins and lush jungle, is also a place of extreme poverty. It is not easily overlooked, particularly when your tuk-tuk ride takes you right past a village of 200 very frail people hit by dengue fever.

Now, by paying for hotels, flights, meals, guides, and local handicrafts, we had already pumped money into the system. But that wasn't a gift; it was an exchange of services and goods and I benefited from it supremely. (You should see my gorgeous gold hoop earrings.)

A sign in our hotel room explained that the hotel sponsored a local orphanage, and if we were interested we could make a donation. We asked our guide whether or not it seemed legit, and he confirmed that the hotel put the funds to good use. So we added up the cost of our hotel bill and made a donation to the orphanage equaling 10 per cent of that sum. The Humanity Tithe.

We try to do something like that everywhere we go. Your contribution does not have to be money. You can bring a laptop or school supplies to a local school, for instance. Or donate air miles.

If you don't know where to start, here are a few pointers: ask your local school or church if they support a sister operation in another country. Find out if a co-worker has connections/ family/interests in programs in the area you are traveling to. Your Facebook feed can be a great place to start: you never know what your network knows. Yes, it's easier to give to an organization like Red Cross, but I like to keep it as local as possible. While the accountability isn't vetted to the same degree, the bureaucracy is much less entrenched.

It's not a major commitment. It's not like voluntourism or starting a foundation or curing cancer. But if you make those your only options for giving, you'll never be in a place to give anything. You can take precious time off, see a remarkable country, and enjoy a truly fun vacation with cocktails and nice sheets, and still contribute in some way to the human experience.

A little real help, donated locally and used immediately, is a great way to express your gratitude. After all, you, the traveler, have been so thoroughly enriched by your host country. Good manners dictate a thank you.

Giving back is a core value at Fathom. We think jetsetting is compatible with do-gooding.

We're inspired by the stories we hear from our community. Of the Manhattan architect who, along with his teenage son, spent a spring break building homes in the Peruvian salt flats. The touring musician who established a music school for children living in an emergency refugee camp in Germany. It's food for thought: what you already know so well can go very far.

Remember, too, that, while your cash donations will have a positive impact, so will your everyday decisions. Support companies with sustainable policies. Buy from local producers. Consider microlending to a collective of women artisans instead of crowdfunding a new suitcase company. Feel like you're invested in the world – wherever you are, because you are – and act accordingly.

Opposite page, top: Bowl of flowers found at a rest stop in Vietnam; opposite page, bottom: boat ride in Bagan, Myanmar; this page, top: Buddhist monks in the making; this page, middle: paddling in Bithoor, India; this page, bottom: installation in Seville, Spain

Volunteer Opportunities Around the Globe

How can we connect with locals? And contribute to the economy? And make new friends? And make some meaning for ourselves? And do so in a dignified manner – without exploiting the environment or the people in it? These are the right questions to ask yourself as you figure out how to travel with a purpose. The world of volunteer travel is a tricky one, but we've found a number of organizations that take great pains to evaluate needs, give assistance with respect, and utilize the traveler's skills and resources to great, positive effect.

Opposite page: Cool is universal: this page: huggable orangutans Ali and Ting Tsan: overleaf page: children splashing around in Thailand

CRUISE WITH A CONSCIENCE DOWN THE AFRICAN COAST

Mission: Mercy Ships' Africa Mercy is a floating hospital that provides medical care to developing countries.

Your job: The ship is like a small city and needs everyone from cooks to teachers to receptionists to keep it running.

Good to know: It's a faith-based organization with a vibrant church scene.

Intensity level: High. But if you think the concept of a traveling hospital is as awesome as we do, this is a cause worth sailing the seven seas for.

mercyships.org
U.S.A.: 1 800 772 7447; International: +1 250 381 2160

GET CLOSE TO ENDANGERED SPECIES

Mission: The Great Projects facilitates trips with local organizations around the world that work with endangered animals through ecofriendly research and rescue missions, in projects as varied as rehabilitating orangutan populations in Borneo and saving tigers on safari in India.

Your job: Provide extra muscle – welding, building, and carpentry skills are a plus.

Good to know: Trips are short term and family friendly, so cancel your beach vacation and save elephants instead.

Intensity level: Medium. The difficulty level depends on the animal and its environment, but staying in beautiful eco-lodges, wildlife conservation centers, and safari parks makes the experience extra special.

thegreatprojects.com
+44 0 208 885 4987

RIDE ON HORSEBACK THROUGH THE INDIAN DESERT

Mission: Relief Riders International provides worldwide humanitarian relief on horseback.

Best for: Horse-riding enthusiasts.

Your job: Ride alongside founder Alexander Souri and his team of doctors and help set up medical camps in small desert villages.

What we love: The extremely unique experience of volunteer and adventure travel.

Good to know: Fast- and slow-paced riding groups are organized. Non-medical volunteers are welcome.

Intensity level: High. It's a unique experience of bonding, immersion, and seeing a side of India you would never experience on a regular tour.

reliefridersinternational.com
+1 413 329 5876

REHABILITATE HAITI

Mission: English in Mind Institute helps Haitian adults find long-term, meaningful employment by teaching them English.

Your job: Spend mornings volunteering at orphanages and afternoons teaching English to adult students.

Good to know: A thing or two about teaching English. It helps if you know French, too.

Intensity level: Medium. Working with non–English speaking children and adults in poverty is intense but so rewarding.

englishinmindinstitute.org

PROTECT MOTHER NATURE IN THE U.S.A.

Mission: Sierra Club builds and maintains trails, parks, and wildlife conservation areas throughout the U.S.

Best for: Outdoorsy types.

Your job: Mother Nature's personal janitor and custodian.

What we love: Pioneer conservationist John Muir founded the organization in 1892, before conservation was even a thing. That's legit.

Good to know: It's the largest and most influential environmental organization in the U.S.

Intensity level: High. Trips involve long hours of outdoor physical labor. But nature is invigorating.

sierraclub.org
+1 415 977 5500

LIFE-CHANGING TIP #09

Doing Good Work and Making a Good Earth

These are a dozen independent non-profit and conservation initiatives that can use our support.

American Prairie Reserve
Creating the largest nature reserve in the U.S.
americanprairie.org

Books for Africa
Collecting and shipping books to students in 54 African countries.
booksforafrica.org

Clean the World
Donating unused hotel toiletries to people who need them.
cleantheworld.org

Ocean Collectiv
Preserving, protecting, and cleaning the world's oceans.
oceancollectiv.co

One Kid, One World
Building schools in Kenya and El Salvador.
onekidoneworld.org

Pachamama Alliance
Empowering and protecting communities in the Amazon rainforest.
pachamama.org

Pencils of Promise
Creating schools and supporting teachers around the world.
pencilsofpromise.org

ShelterBox USA
Providing homes for people displaced by natural disaster and conflict around the world.
shelterboxusa.org

Spark Ventures
Providing business know-how to raise communities out of poverty.
sparkventures.org

The Ocean Cleanup
Ridding the seas of plastic.
theoceancleanup.com

The Small Things
Empowering families in Tanzania.
thesmallthings.org

We Are Family Foundation
Empowers and mentors young global citizens who are positively changing the world.
wearefamily foundation.org

BUILD COMMUNITY IN THAILAND
Mission: Local Alike creates economic growth and employment opportunities in rural Thailand through community-based tourism and cultural exchange.
Your job: Support villages through cross-cultural engagement.
Good to know: Various activities are led by people in the communities: mountain climbing, camping, tours, etc.
Intensity level: Low. Camping and trekking trips are more intense than village stays. You can expect hot water in some places, but forget about wifi.

localalike.com
+66 81 139 5593

EMPOWER ECONOMIES
Mission: Foundation for Sustainable Development trains students and professionals while providing support to partner NGOs in developing countries.
Your job: Engage in community-specific issues (environment, economy) and monitor their efficacy.
Good to know: ProCorps volunteer trips are for professionals with five-plus years of experience in a specific area of focus. Global Service Trips are short-term group trips organized through local partners.
Intensity level: Medium. Programs are immersive and can last up to a year.

fsd.org
+1 415 283 4873

DIVE IN WITH ENDANGERED MARINE LIFE

Mission: Oceanic Society deepens the connection between people and the ocean through conservation and travel programs.

Your job: Accompany scientists on sea-bound research expeditions – whale-watching, polar cruises, snorkeling adventures, and wildlife encounters.

Good to know: Expeditions are all over the world, concentrated mainly throughout the Pacific.

Intensity level: Low. Explore local environments and monitor marine life.

oceanicsociety.org
U.S.A.: 1 800 326 7491; International: +1 415 256 9604

MAKE COMMUNITY SERVICE THE NEW NORMAL

Mission: Projects Abroad encourages young people to volunteer for worthwhile causes to make society more service-minded.

Your job: Be an extra set of hands, whether you're interning at a human rights NGO in Argentina, teaching English as a foreign language, or coaching children's sports teams.

Good to know: The most popular programs are the Care Projects, which involve working with children at orphanages and day-care centers.

Intensity level: Varied. Long-term trips involve certifications; Alternative Spring Break trips are great for college students; Global Gap Year options for recent grads are endless.

projects-abroad.org
1 212 244 7234

Rays of light in Son
Đong District, Vietnam

PART VIII

When Your Hotel Is the Destination

Home Away from Home

Boy, do we love great hotels. They're our home away from home and the anchor of just about any trip we plan. Sometimes, the hotel is the reason for the trip. There have been more than a few times when a destination rose to the top of our must-go list because an incredible feat of engineering or hospitality – or both – started drawing visitors from near and far.

Of course, a hotel is, in its essence, a place to lay your head and take a shower in peace. But it can also be a refuge after a long and exhausting flight, a portal into a new way of living, a window into a different culture, a space to rejuvenate, or the way to pretend that you live somewhere new and altogether different, amid impeccable design, crisp white sheets, and French fries on demand from 24-hour room service. Good hotels meet a traveler's most basic needs of cleanliness, safety, and shelter, but great hotels anticipate guest needs at every turn, reflect (or transcend) the destination they are in, and make it hard to leave.

The global hotel scene is massive and always evolving, a living, breathing organism that adapts to reflect its surroundings and ever-changing traveler demands. While big-name hotel chains can reflect larger travel trends, we get most excited about the boutique hotels – independent passion projects, old classics that have been revamped, local hangouts, and hidden gems.

Perhaps the most influential hotel in recent times has been The Ace Hotel (see the entry later in this chapter), for the way it transformed the lobby concept, tweaking it from the traditional (check-in desk, anonymous seating area, elevator music) into a more welcoming, mixed-use space – a cool coffee shop, a handsomely weathered workspace, a buzzy restaurant, a cocktail-forward bar, and an indie music venue. By doing so, Ace helped redefine the hotel, transforming it from a place strictly for tourists into a bustling neighborhood building block designed as much for locals as for visitors.

Fifty years ago, chain hotels delivered a consistent experience regardless of destination, so that a loyal Hilton or Holiday Inn guest knew what they were getting, from Houston to Rome to Beijing. Today, the pendulum has swung in the opposite direction, as hotels – even the big chains – strive to imbue as much local character as possible into their offerings, aiming to become destinations in their own right, sometimes by opening on the bleeding edge of new neighborhoods.

The compilation of hotels on the following pages lists just a few (really!) of the standouts the Fathom team knows and loves for so many reasons. For their innovative design. For their memorable origin stories. For their thoughtful services and amenities. For sheer old-fashioned romance. For cool atmospheres at affordable prices. For the lovely people in charge.

Among the goodies you'll find a surrealist vineyard retreat, a hyper-modern hotel on a remote archipelago, a 230-year-old fortress–turned–luxury estate, and a village of historic dwellings transported to the suburbs. You'll know you're in for something special as soon as you roll your suitcase up to the check-in counter, even if it's just a sweet host with an iPad and a fresh juice.

Opposite page: Hotel
San Cristóbal in Todos
Santos, Mexico

Architectural Feats

The future is closer than you think. Traditional structures, like castles and estates, will always have their place, but forward-thinking hoteliers are looking ahead, commissioning architects and designers to build for the next generation using unconventional materials and innovative techniques.

FOGO ISLAND INN
Fogo Island, Newfoundland, Canada

This hyper-modern hotel on a remote, rugged archipelago is a treat for the eye. Local architect Todd Saunders built a saltbox-inspired structure with solar panels and steel stilts, lifting 29 rooms up from the craggy moors and rogue Arctic ice floes. Many furnishings were handcrafted, in homage to disappearing arts. The kitchen staff seasonally forages for dinner, and just might invite you to their home afterwards. Other sleek touches include in-room wood-burning stoves and hot tubs on the roof. All surplus from the inn is reinvested back into the community. How's that for sustainability?

fogoislandinn.ca
210 Main Road, Joe Batt's Arm
+1 855 268 9277

Opposite page: Fogo Island Inn; this page, top: the roof deck; this page, bottom: the dining room

SHIPWRECK LODGE
Skeleton Coast, Namibia

For a one-of-a-kind adventure, this striking hotel in the remote north-west region of Namibia is set in some of the most arresting landscapes on the continent. Inspired by the shipwrecks that line the country's Atlantic coast (the bushmen named it The Land God Made in Anger), the ship's cabin–style bedrooms feel like a respite from the elements, especially once you get under the thick faux-fur covers with a hot water bottle. Designed by a Namibian team comprised of architect Nina Maritz and interior designer Melanie van der Merwe, the solar-powered abodes were built with the environment in mind, using only timber nails. Daytime activities include game drives, climbing sand dunes to watch the desert sun rise, and visiting the mysterious *Suiderkus* and *Karimona* shipwreck remnants.

shipwrecklodge.com.na
Skeleton Coast Park Mowe Bay
+264 61 228 104

AMANYANGYUN
Shanghai, China

Over a 15-year period, an endangered village of historic dwellings and 1000-year-old camphor trees were preserved and transported more than 400 miles (644 kilometers) to Shanghai's Minhang District. Kerry Hill Architects then painstakingly restored the disassembled homes, converting them into guest accommodations. Also on site is a modern-day re-creation of a 17th-century Chinese scholar's studio, where guests can spend time learning, contemplating, and practicing traditional crafts like calligraphy, music, and painting.

aman.com
6161 Yuanjiang Road, Minhang District
+86 21 8011 9999

Opposite page: Punta Caliza;
this page, top: Shipwreck
Lodge; this page, bottom:
Amanyangun

PUNTA CALIZA
Isla Holbox, Mexico

A Mexican architect and his artist wife created a 12-room oasis on Isla Holbox, an increasingly trendy island near Cancun. They built it with cedar from their tree farm, which was planted in the birth year of their firstborn son, who now helps manage the hotel with his sister. The design reinterprets ancient Mayan architecture through a sustainable, contemporary lens. Instead of a traditional Mayan courtyard, a shallow triangular pool anchors the property, surrounded by thatched-roofed huts that contain the guest rooms, each with their own private plunge pool that connects to the main one. You can swim right up to your room.

puntacaliza.com
77310 Isla Holbox, Quintana Roo
+52 99 8800 0119

Hostels That Look Like Boutique Hotels

Bad lighting, sterile dormitories, and pay-as-you-rinse showers are nowhere to be found in these hostels. Nowadays, young hoteliers and smart entrepreneurs are responding to millennials' love of new experiences, good design, and community spaces with budget hotels that are affordable luxuries: friendly, social, wifi-equipped, and ready for your next photo op.

THE INDEPENDENTE HOSTEL & SUITES
Lisbon, Portugal
Spacious and bright in a picturesque city square, this former residence has 100-year-old moldings, modern furniture, beautiful floor tiles, and suites with balconies overlooking the river. Perks: security cards, lockers, and a cool restaurant and bar serving Portuguese fare. Private rooms? Yes: suites with classical Portuguese architecture.

theindependente.pt
Rua de São Pedro de Alcântara, nº 81
+351 21 346 1381

NATIVE HOSTEL BAR & KITCHEN
Austin, Texas, U.S.A.
The industrial design is so elegant, you'll wonder if you've stumbled into the coolest boutique hotel in town. Guests can choose from communal rooms outfitted with bunk beds and a shared bath, loft rooms with bunk beds and one king-sized bed (ideal for larger groups), or private suites. And what with weekday happy hour, DJ sets, yoga, tubing excursions, and movie screenings, you'll never be at a loss for something cool to do.

nativehostels.com
807 E 4th Street
+1 512 551 9947

Opposite page: The Independente Hostel & Suites; this page: Native Hostel Bar & Kitchen; overleaf page: Kaisu in Tokyo

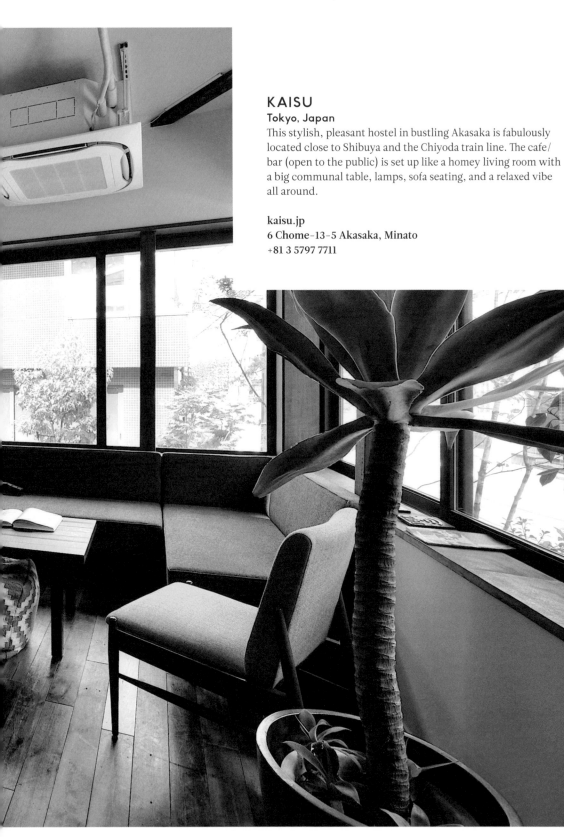

KAISU
Tokyo, Japan
This stylish, pleasant hostel in bustling Akasaka is fabulously located close to Shibuya and the Chiyoda train line. The cafe/bar (open to the public) is set up like a homey living room with a big communal table, lamps, sofa seating, and a relaxed vibe all around.

kaisu.jp
6 Chome-13-5 Akasaka, Minato
+81 3 5797 7711

Opposite page: Caveland; this page, top left: Reykjavik; this page, top right: Downtown Beds' design-forward bunks; this page, bottom left: matching in Marrakech; this page, bottom right: Caveland

EQUITY POINT MARRAKECH
Marrakech, Morocco
Save the haggling for the vendors in Place Jemaa el-Fnaa. This little oasis in the center of town has all the charm of a classic riad without the luxury hotel price tag. Guests swim in the courtyard pool and dine on the terrace to the sound of live Moroccan music. Off-campus activities include souk tours, traditional cooking classes, and journeys into the desert.

equity-point.com
80, Derb El Hammam Mouassine
+34 93 231 20 45

KEX
Reykjavik, Iceland
A converted biscuit factory that's cozy and hip, just two blocks from the city's main drag. Reclaimed wood floors, Bauhaus furniture, and lots of books make the gastropub, lively bar, and heated patio places to linger. Accommodations are a mix of private, shared, and family-style. The extras include movie premieres, art parties, a barbershop, a gym, and free wifi.

kexhostel.is
Skúlagata 28
+354 561 6060

CAVELAND
Santorini, Greece

True to the site's original architecture and design, the grotto of this 18th-century winery-turned-hostel is carved into 3600-year-old volcanic pumice. Lemon, pomegranate, and pistachio trees grow everywhere, lending a lushness to the stone and woodwork painted in hues of aqua. Relax by one of the island's largest swimming pools, then retreat to the private historic apartment, girls-only caves, or double rooms.

cave-land.com
Post Box 39, Karterádos
+30 22860 22122

DOWNTOWN BEDS
Mexico City, Mexico

Old palaces are adapted for all sorts of modern-day uses, but Spanish nobility never could have guessed that their grand Mexican palace would be repurposed as social hostels for the young and mobile. Here, tidy bunk beds feel more like private pods thanks to nice design decisions. Clever amenities are stashed throughout: laundry on the rooftop, a pool on the terrace, beer on the patio, hammocks and bicycles at the ready. Trailblazing hotel company Grupo Habita owns several boutique hotels throughout Mexico and the U.S., and they bring the same fun and fearless sensibility to their down-market offering.

downtownbeds.com
Calle Isabel la Católica 30, Centro Histórico, Centro
+52 55 5130 6855

Hotels for Instagram Addicts

When you're not trying to style the perfect overhead food shot or capture the sunset through a glass of Champagne, you're making friends jealous of the gorgeous bedroom interiors from your travels. Bright rooms, bold patterns, and lots of cozy details make these boutique hotels worth visiting for the Instagram shot alone. #TravelWithFathom #NoFilterNeeded

ETT HEM
Stockholm, Sweden

A dreamy Scandinavian townhouse has been converted from an elegant home into this 12-room boutique hotel. Thoughtful touches like cashmere blankets and potted plants have been strewn about by London-based designer Ilse Crawford, creating a warm and welcoming environment. Old-world details like original molding and velvet couches mix with modern amenities like rain showers and Michael Anastassiades lights. The especially photogenic Ulf Nordfjell–designed garden is a great place to curl up with a glass of wine and snack from the equally picturesque kitchen.

etthem.se
Sköldungagatan 2, SE-114 27
+46 8 200590

LINE DC
Washington, D.C., U.S.A.

Hallelujah. Everyone who comes through town should pay their respects to this stunning hotel in a 110-year-old Neoclassical church located in the diverse and always-buzzing Adams Morgan neighborhood. The community-led effort (by local chefs, artists, and designers) shows: the 220-room hotel has a decidedly Washingtonian look, with lobby seating from repurposed mahogany pews, salvaged hymnal pages adapted as art, and 60-foot (18-meter) vaulted ceilings aiming for the high heavens. The hotel lobby is home to Full Service Radio, a local talk-radio station created by Heritage Radio alum Jack Inslee.

thelinehotel.com
1770 Euclid Street NW
+1 202 588 0525

Opposite page: Line DC; this page, top: Ett Hem courtyard; this page, bottom: Ett Hem library

Opposite page: Zero
George; this page, top:
Halcyon House; this page,
bottom: the pool at Hotel
Saint Cecilia

HALCYON HOUSE
Cabarita Beach, Australia

Move over, Byron Bay. The cool crowd is heading up the Gold
Coast to Cabarita Beach, a seaside town with wide beaches and
terrific surf. This former motel's original 1960s architecture
and chill vibes have been preserved and given an of-the-
moment style update – and a fresh coat of white and blue
paint. Bright patterns cover everything, from the upholstered
walls to the pillowcases to the handmade tiles in the bathroom,
plus carefully curated antiques and a dizzying collection of
paintings and wall hangings make every room feel special. The
sunny restaurant is also a draw, as are the pool and the bar.

halcyonhouse.com.au
21 Cypress Crescent
+61 02 6676 1444

HOTEL SAINT CECILIA
Austin, Texas, U.S.A.

Lived-in chesterfield couches, chandeliers hanging from trees,
and an old Citroën permanently parked on the property are
just a few charming touches at the property that launched
influential hotelier Liz Lambert to hospitality stardom. Named
after the patron saint of music and poetry, this small hotel
(three studios, six poolside bungalows) also has five suites
inspired by pop-culture icons. We like the idea of bathing in a
private, bamboo-lined outdoor shower in the Patti Smith suite,
but the Instagram-famous swimming pool is also compelling.

hotelsaintcecilia.com
112 Academy Drive
+1 512 852 2400

ZERO GEORGE
Charleston, South Carolina, U.S.A.

With an accent as slow as molasses and Charleston charm
with a capital C, this small and chic inn is comprised of three
perfectly aged 1804 residences and two carriage houses
connected by a cozy, palmetto-shaded courtyard. Heart pine
flooring, traditional millwork, and wicker furniture give the
space a bygone vibe. A shiny fleet of pistachio-colored bicycles
beckon riders to get on the saddle and ride.

zerogeorge.com
0 George Street
+1 843 817 7900

WYTHE HOTEL
Brooklyn, New York, U.S.A.
This old factory on the waterfront epitomizes New Brooklyn style. It's cool, laidback but high-end, and topped with a rooftop bar. With its industrial-chic furnishings (poured concrete floors, exposed red brick walls), floor-to-ceiling windows facing Manhattan over the East River, and the beautiful floor tiles in Reynard restaurant, it is no surprise that this 1901 building is one of the 'Gram's original darlings.

wythehotel.com
80 Wythe Avenue
+1 718 460 8000

AMERICAN TRADE HOTEL
Panama City, Panama
This restoration project – a collaboration between Atelier Ace (of Ace Hotels), Commune Design, and Conservatorio, a local development agency – put Panama's historic neighborhood on the radar of design-minded travelers. Its aesthetic is multi-layered, with touches that span the structure's 340-year history: Bertoia side chairs mix with potted plants, textile art, and wooden floors made from sunken logs from the famous canal.

americantradehotel.com
Plaza Herrera Casco Viejo
+507 211 2000

HOTEL SAN CRISTÓBAL
Todos Santos, Mexico
For the visually inclined, this beachfront boutique hotel feels like something out of a dream. Set against the backdrop of an emerald-green pool and the deep-blue Pacific, the decor features vibrant patterned concrete tiles intermixed with colorful textiles and furniture. Bright-pink inner tubes rest on the surface of the pool while guests wearing the hotel's signature striped robes lounge in the shade of white umbrellas.

sancristobalbaja.com
Playa Punta Lobos, Carretera Federal N°19, Km 54+800
U.S.A.: 1 855 227 1535; International: 011 52 612 175 1530

Opposite page: The Whitby Hotel; this page, top: Wythe Hotel; this page, middle: American Trade Hotel; this page, bottom: Hotel San Cristóbal

THE WHITBY HOTEL
New York, New York, U.S.A.

Who said midtown Manhattan had to be all business and all boring? Leave it to English hotelier and design director Kit Kemp to infuse the neighborhood with her bright and patterned carefree style. Guest rooms impress with floor-to-ceiling windows, unique color schemes, and just a touch of British eccentricity. Meals can be taken in The Orangery, an eclectic dining room filled with illuminated porcelain pots depicting NYC landmarks. The lobby, hallways, and public spaces are filled with an impressive, global-minded collection of contemporary art. That reimagined grandfather clock by the elevator? It's watching you.

firmdalehotels.com
18 W 56th Street
+1 212 586 5656

Hotels with Former Lives

For many people, travel is about transformation and reinvention. Why not also hotels, especially in an era committed to reuse and recycling? As our surroundings evolve, it's important to know where we've been. For every gleaming new tower that pierces tomorrow's skyline, there's a lesson to be learned from yesterday's demolition. We applaud the creativity that went into converting fortresses, prisons, and firehouses into attention-worthy inns.

ALILA FORT BISHANGARH
Jaipur, India

It took seven years to turn a 230-year-old hilltop fortress into a retreat in rural Rajasthan on the road between Delhi and Jaipur. Old meets new in the ancient turrets and walls that still have their openings for firearms, and in the modern offerings in 59 suites and several on-site restaurants. If you get invited down to the former dungeon, say yes. It's now the spa.

alilahotels.com
Off NH-8 at Manoharpur
+91 723 005 8058

THE LIBERTY HOTEL
Boston, Massachusetts, U.S.A.

"Liberty" is an ironic name for the luxury Beacon Hill hotel that spent its first 140 years as Beantown's prison. But the revamp is striking, as seen in the circular windows and balconies in the four-story atrium lobby, as well as dynamic, making the hotel a destination for eating and drinking (including at – har, har – Clink), shopping, and, oh yes, sleeping.

libertyhotel.com
215 Charles Street
+1 617 224 4000

Opposite page: A balcony at 1898 The Post; this page, top: Alila Fort Bishangarh; this page, bottom: The Liberty Hotel

LIFE-CHANGING TIP #10

Five-Fingered Souvenirs

You love them in your hotel room, and even more when you smuggle them home. A silver ashtray here. A fancy monogrammed towel there. Swiping hotel amenities is a long-held tradition among the traveling set. You'll get charged for some of these, but items this lovely are too hard to resist.

BELMOND HOTEL DAS CATARATAS
Parque Nacional Iguazú, Brazil
Granado toiletries from the storied Rio apothecary.
belmond.com

J.K. PLACE
Florence, Italy
A fantastic city guide curated by general manager Claudio Meli.
jkplace.com

THE RITZ
London, England
Plush, navy blue slippers.
theritzlondon.com

LE SIRENUSE
Positano, Italy
Custom-scented Eau D'Italie toiletries.
sirenuse.it

PULITZER
Amsterdam, The Netherlands
Tiny bicycle repair kit.
pulitzeramsterdam.com

SHANGRI-LA BARR AL JISSAH
Muscat, Oman
Traditional Omani coffee cups for drinking Arabic coffee.
shangri-la.com

KASBAH TAMADOT
Asni, Morocco
Soft Moroccan leather babouches.
virginlimitededition.com

AMANZOE
Kranidi, Greece
Straw hat, flip flops, and beach bag provided for the beach club.
aman.com

THE RITZ-CARLTON
Koh Samui, Thailand
Bottles of bug spray made in-house from citronella, eucalyptus, and neem essential oils.
ritzcarlton.com

1898 THE POST
Ghent, Belgium
Housed on the top two floors of a former post office with a striking neo-Gothic facade, the small boutique hotel is decorated with dark colors, antique furniture, and large windows overlooking the city. Days start with a delicious homemade breakfast and cup of tea in The Kitchen, a relaxed open-format restaurant with cozy upholstered seating in neutral tones.

zannierhotels.com
Graslei 16
+32 9 277 09 60

DETROIT FOUNDATION HOTEL
Detroit, Michigan, U.S.A.
Everybody is rooting for Detroit, and the city's revitalization is a long time coming. Until recently, it has been slim pickings for the hotel scene, until a historic fire department headquarters became a thoughtfully designed 100-room independent hotel and love letter to the city. Local distillers, brewers, farmers, and manufacturers have been brought together to deliver an authentic Detroit experience centered around builders and makers. In-house restaurant The Chef's Table doubles as an incubator for the city's emerging talent.

detroitfoundationhotel.com
250 W Larned Street
+1 313 800 5500

Opposite page: 1898 The Post; this page, top: El
Cosmico; this page, bottom: El Cosmico

EL COSMICO
Marfa, Texas, U.S.A.

Charm abounds at this bohemian trailer park. The
tiny, isolated art town of Marfa, a.k.a. the Middle
of Nowhere, West Texas, has drawn overworked
vagabonds time and again for a much-needed
reset. Thirteen beautifully restored 1950s-era
mobile homes are the main draw – though there
are also teepees, seasonal yurts, and safari-
style tents on the campground. Without the
distraction of TV, telephones, or internet access
(except in the lounge), you can channel your
inner creative at a workshop or while away the
hours talking about existential matters under
vast, star-filled skies.

elcosmico.com
802 West Highland Avenue
+1 877 822 1950

Cheaper Than It Should Be

If money were no object, booking travel would be a cinch. But when time and cash are in short supply – and good taste and high style still matter – searching for an affordable (or even cheap) hotel that's also a pleasure to stay in can feel like looking for a needle in a haystack. Do cool, quirky, clever, and charming budget hotels even exist? Yes, they do.

ACE HOTEL SEATTLE
Seattle, Washington, U.S.A.

The original hipster hotel, opened before hipsters were even a thing, occupies a former inn for maritime laborers from the historic waterfront district. It set a standard that countless others have since followed: minimalist design, reclaimed hardwood flooring, eco touches, and artwork by graffiti giant Shepard Fairey. The cool Pacific Northwest vibe is all its own.

acehotel.com
2423 First Avenue
+1 206 448 4721

CATAHOULA HOTEL
New Orleans, Louisiana, U.S.A.

The 35-room restored Creole townhouse is a modern escape with a touch of patina. Rooms are simple but sleek, with white linens, modern furniture, and a few intricate details (custom-made vanities from Louisiana cypress wood, soothing rainfall shower heads). The bar serves an array of pisco-based cocktails, while the restaurant offers a globally inspired menu.

catahoulahotel.com
914 Union Street
+1 504 603 2422

SIR SAVIGNY HOTEL
Berlin, Germany

An Art Deco urban retreat for modern aristocrats (on a budget) located in the luxe Charlottenburg neighborhood. Sleek wooden finishes, leather furniture, and eclectic art accentuate a warm, friendly vibe. Rooms come with a twist – a burger intercom connecting hungry guests to The Butcher restaurant located downstairs.

sirhotels.com
Kantstraße 144
+49 (0)30 323 015 671

Opposite page: Casa Bonay; this page, top: Catahoula Hotel; this page, bottom: Sir Savigny Hotel

Poolside at Austin Motel in Texas

AUSTIN MOTEL
Austin, Texas, U.S.A.

The motel's motto says it all: "So close, yet so far out." Vibrant colors and attention-grabbing wallpaper adorn guest rooms in a style as unapologetically playful as it is effortlessly cool, while the kidney-shaped pool in the center of the property and surrounding lido deck are Instagram heaven. The original 1930s sign at the entrance, still standing, is the inspiration behind the vintage aesthetic, along with design hints from the '50s (color scheme) and '80s (artwork).

austinmotel.com
1220 S Congress Avenue
+1 512 441 1157

ALABAMA HOTEL
Hobart, Australia

A 19th-century pub with rooms to let has been reimagined as a hip budget boutique hotel in a city prized for its indie sensibility. A plant-filled balcony, nicely stocked bar, vintage touches, tidy rooms, free wifi, and a very friendly staff make for a great escape down under.

alabamahobart.com.au
72 Liverpool Street
+61 499 987 698

THE ROBEY
Chicago, Illinois, U.S.A.

Continuing Grupo Habita's tradition of repurposing old structures in clever, contemporary ways, this hotel's Art Deco designs are fused with midcentury modern furniture in a sleek, minimalist palette of lights and darks, resulting in a self-professed "confident mix of Americana." Two watering holes and a triangular rooftop pool round out the offerings on the border of Wicker Park and Bucktown.

therobey.com
2018 W North Avenue
+1 872 315 3050

Opposite page, top: Brown Beach House Croatia; opposite page, bottom: Casa Mae; this page, top: Austin Motel; this page, bottom: Alabama Hotel

BROWN BEACH HOUSE CROATIA
Trogir, Croatia

There is nothing budget about the sophisticated design furnishings of this 42-room boutique property in a charming seaside town with Renaissance and Romanesque touches. There's a full spa, a pretty sun terrace, a lively breakfast scene, and an Instagram-worthy pool with a view of the Adriatic coast. On rainy days (of which there are very few), it feels just as vacation-y to spend a few hours indoors, in the spacious, well-appointed parlor equipped with cozy couches, an eclectic array of books, discreet toys for kids, and excellent coffee and cocktails.

brownhotels.com
Put Gradine 66
+385 21 355 450

CASA MAE
Lagos, Portugal

This 19th-century family estate is now a 33-room boutique hotel oozing Portuguese tranquilidade, with terracotta flooring and traditional wooden reixa on the façade. A self-published design magazine, curated artisan boutique, and open-kitchen restaurant make it more than just a place to lay your head.

casa-mae.com
Rua do Jogo da Bola 41
+351 968 369 732

THE HOXTON,
Williamsburg, U.S.A.

Rooms are 'Cosy' or 'Roomy' (and feel like jewel boxes) and the adorable living room lobby encourages guests and locals alike to work, eat, and play. The look is retro-industrial with a feminine twist — from the show kitchen to the outdoor amphitheater and party space that feels like a cool Brooklyn apartment.

thehoxton.com
97 Wythe Avenue
+1 718 215 7100

TRIBAL HOTEL
Granada, Nicaragua

A beautifully decorated boho outpost in the sleepy colonial city of Granada, the cutest town in Nicaragua. The seven-room hotel is as authentic as can be, with tables, chairs, handmade tiles, and pool loungers made by local blacksmiths, fabricators, and woodworkers. The place is low-key and tropical, totally in line with the country's modest vibe.

tribal-hotel.com
Calle Cuiscoma
+505 2552 0037

CASA BONAY
Barcelona, Spain

A perfect escape set in a 19th-century Neoclassical building in peaceful Dreta de l'Eixample. The simple palette of whites, blues, and greens complements the interior's original mosaic floors, while a collection of local purveyors – like Catalan baristas Satan's Coffee Corner and indie publishers Blackie Books – adds a special touch to the common spaces.

casabonay.com
Gran Via de les Corts Catalanes, 700
+34 935 45 80 50

MOXY OSAKA HONMACHI
Osaka, Japan

A hip home away from home thoughtfully designed with dynamic artwork that captures the bustle of the surrounding city. The hotel lounge has the vibe of a coffee shop during the day and a clubby atmosphere for drinks at night. A 24-hour self-service cafe and grocer, speedy wifi, and an assortment of workspaces and games make managing a late arrival and fighting jet lag a breeze.

marriott.com
2-2-9 Kawaramachi, Chuo-ku
+81 6 6204 5200

Tribal Hotel

LIFE-CHANGING TIP #11

In Praise of the Mini Chains

These hit machines of the boutique hotel industry manage to keep their cool by adapting old buildings, reflecting their respective destinations through services and design, drawing the local crowd, and delivering charm through nice extras – like incredibly affordable nightly rates.

Generator Hostels

Major cities from Amsterdam to Miami

Old warehouses and factory buildings are reimagined as gathering spots for cool kids who don't want to be called backpackers. Quirky interiors mirror the neighborhood, with lots of design details to keep eyes wandering. Bedroom types range from shared to private.
generatorhostels.com

Mama Shelter

Global capitals from Belgrade and Bordeaux to Los Angeles and Rio

Cute and contemporary and Philippe Starck–designed, with a minimalist look and fun-to-the-max vibe. Perks include video booths, iMacs, free wifi, free movies, events, and quirky in-room items. Private rooms are available with ensuite bathrooms.
mamashelter.com

Freehand

Chicago, Los Angeles, Miami, and New York

Eclectic and funky interiors draw a reliably fun and fashionable crowd. As they function as both hotels and hostels, guests can choose from private rooms with ensuite bathrooms or shared rooms with hotel-grade mattresses. Even if you're not staying here, drop by for a drink at The Broken Shaker.
freehandhotels.com

21c Museum Hotels

American cities, primarily in the South

Their first hotel, located along Museum Mile in Louisville, Kentucky, helped launch the art-in-hotels trend that rages on. With their additional outposts throughout the region, the company is helping to fuel the American Southern revival, still going strong. In addition to artwork in their modern rooms, every hotel is also a contemporary art museum (free and open to the public) with rotating exhibitions, as well as a chef-driven restaurant.
21cmuseumhotels.com

Storied Stays

Hemingway knew how to get out of town. Wilde knew how to take up residence. And Capote knew how to throw a damn fine hotel party. Follow in the footsteps of famous authors, rest your head at their favorite hotel haunts, and kickstart your imagination.

THE ALGONQUIN
New York, New York, U.S.A.
During the Roaring Twenties, a group of witty critics, playwrights, magazine founders, Pulitzer Prize winners, and writers (like Dorothy Parker, Ruth Hale, and Alexander Woollcott) met every day at this New York City hotel for lunch, games, wisecracks, and lots of gin.

algonquinhotel.com
59 West 44th Street
+1 212 840 6800

HOTEL AMBOS MUNDOS
Havana, Cuba
Ernest Hemingway began writing *For Whom the Bell Tolls* in room 551 of the Old Havana hotel, where he lived for seven years before relocating to the hills outside the city. If you want to go up to see his old digs, which have been converted into a mini museum, be a sport and tip the elevator guy.

gaviotahotels.com
153 Obispo
+53 7860 9530

Opposite page: GoldenEye Hotel & Resort; this page, top: Manhattan skyscrapers; this page, bottom: Hotel Ambos Mundos

L'HOTEL
Paris, France

Oscar Wilde lived and died in room 16 of the five-star Paris hotel when he was 20,000 francs in debt. Argentine writer Jorge Luis Borges, a Wilde fan, checked in for quiet writing time. Both would be impressed that the hotel maintains its theatrical allure, from garden restaurant to basement hammam, still inspiring louche living.

l-hotel.com
13 Rue des Beaux Arts
+33 1 4441 9900

THE SAVOY
London, England

Chaucer began writing *The Canterbury Tales* here in the 1300s when it was the Savoy Palace. Poet William Blake spent the last years of his life across the alley. In 1889, a Gilbert & Sullivan producer opened the luxury hotel, which soon became a favorite of Oscar Wilde and Noël Coward, among others. Today, the hotel's Literary Ambassador oversees the Writer-in-Residence program, the in-house Book Butler, and regularly hosts literary salons.

fairmont.com/savoy
Strand
+44 0 20 7836 4343

Opposite page: Room with a view at GoldenEye; this page, top: L'Hotel; this page, middle: Kaspar's at The Savoy; this page, bottom: bathtime at GoldenEye

GOLDENEYE HOTEL & RESORT
Oracabessa, Jamaica

Former intelligence officer Ian Fleming expatriated to Jamaica after a military mission in the Caribbean. Built a villa on an idyllic patch along the beach in the banana port town of Oracabessa. Called it GoldenEye, after a secret WWII mission. And penned the entire James Bond series here.

goldeneye.com
Oracabessa Bay, St. Mary
+1 876 622 9009

Most Romantic Hotels

The world, it turns out, is a very romantic place. Private islands in just about every ocean. Hilltop retreats with views to infinity. Seemingly endless stretches of white sand beaches. Curtains billowing in the breeze around four-poster beds. Being in the mood for love is only the beginning. Being in the right place for love is the clincher.

VILLA FELTRINELLI
Lake Garda, Italy

It may not be as well known as Lake Como, and that's all the better if your idea of amore involves a sumptuous, 19th-century lakefront villa with a long (and at times notorious) history. Much as you'll want to gaze into your companion's eyes, you might be distracted by the restored antiques, the centuries-old lemon trees, and your Michelin-starred meal on the pergola. Don't fight it. You're in Italy: you're supposed to be in love with everything you see.

villafeltrinelli.com
Via Rimembranza 38–40, Gargnano
+39 0365 79 80 00

LONGITUDE 131°
Uluru, Australia

The hotel is the only place where you can sit in your luxe tented pavilion or under the stars and look directly at Uluru (Ayers Rock) and, from the dunetop, Kata Tjuta (The Olgas), both significant sacred Aboriginal sites and World Heritage–listed natural icons. It's the epitome of what they call "privilege of place."

longitude131.com.au
Yulara Drive, Yulara
+61 2 9918 4355

Opposite page:
A view for two at Villa Feltrinelli; this page, top: restaurant at Villa Feltrinelli; this page, bottom: overlooking Longitude 131°

DELAIRE GRAFF LODGES AND SPA
Stellenbosch, South Africa

If it's privacy, good wine, and a beautiful setting you're after, look no further than the intimate estate nestled in the Cape winelands' scenic Helshoogte Mountain pass, amid the area's many vineyards. The view from your private plunge pool: now that's one to savor. A state-of-the-art winery, two outstanding restaurants, diamond boutique, and excellent spa make for an ideal romantic getaway.

delaire.co.za
Helshoogte Pass
+27 21 885 8160

LA RÉSERVE PARIS HOTEL & SPA
Paris, France

This is the place to live your if-I-were-French-royalty fantasies. The mansion, mere steps from the Grand Palais in the eighth arrondissement, was originally home to the Duc de Morny (Napoléon III's half brother) and more recently to designer Pierre Cardin. Its hotel incarnation retains the lavish opulence, with antiques and silks and marbles and paintings filling the intimate public spaces and 40 light-filled suites and rooms. The excellent spa in the basement, infused with warm red light, has a pool – a rarity in Paris – and the two-Michelin-starred restaurant will provide some of the best meals you'll have in town. Your only challenge will be leaving.

lareserve-paris.com
42 Avenue Gabriel
+33 1 58 36 60 60

Opposite page: Villa TreVille; this page, top: Delaire Graff Lodges and Spa; this page, middle: La Réserve; this page, bottom: the pool at La Réserve

VILLA TREVILLE
Positano, Italy

This stunning former seaside estate of Italian director Franco Zeffirelli is set in lush gardens on the Amalfi Coast. Just as dramatic are the in-room design details (hand-painted herringbone tiling, whimsical mosaics, mother-of-pearl furniture) and fruit-laden cocktails served in the Salone Bianca. The service is fabulous – wholly unobtrusive, completely attentive. The best of Italy in all respects.

villatreville.com
Via Arienzo, 30
+39 089 812 2411

Glamping Holidays

Woodsy retreats elicit memories of campfire s'mores, cabin songs, and figuring out how to get the daddy longlegs out of the shower. But that was before "glamping" was even a word. Proving that not all camping is created equal, today's tents look like boutique hotels, outfitted with luxury linens, modern technology, and top-notch services. As many places are only open seasonally, it's best to inquire about reservation availability before delving too deep into your travel planning.

VENTANA BIG SUR
Big Sur, California, U.S.A.
With views of the glistening Pacific and surrounding valley, this iconic NorCal hippie retreat has some of the finest accommodations around, including 15 safari-style canvas tents with custom-designed glamping mattresses and lush linens, a wood-burning firepit, electric lamps, power outlets with USB ports for charging devices, and access to the main resort's offerings.

ventanabigsur.com
48123 Highway 1
+1 800 628 6500

Opposite page: Under Canvas Mount Rushmore; this page, top: a room at Ventana Big Sur; this page, bottom: Wild Coast Tented Lodge

WILD COAST TENTED LODGE
Yala, Sri Lanka

Built on a stretch of land adjacent to the leopard-roamed Yala National Park, cocoon-like tents crafted from natural materials seamlessly blend into the surrounding landscape. You will not want for creature comforts – there's air conditioning, four-poster beds, and handmade copper bathtubs. Along with an always-changing menu of fine Sri Lankan cuisine and an enormous free-form swimming pool, there are wilderness tours and spa treatments to fill the days.

resplendentceylon.com
Yala National Park
+94 11 774 5730

UNDER CANVAS MOUNT RUSHMORE
Keystone, South Dakota, U.S.A.

Located on the outskirts of an old gold mining settlement between Badlands National Park and Black Hills National Forest, this glampsite offers stylish safari-inspired canvas tents with connected bathrooms and showers. The restaurant, also in an elaborate tent, serves leisurely breakfasts and pioneer-inspired dinners. Activities run the gamut from tame (panning for gold and a buffalo safari jeep tour) to adventurous (horseback riding and rock climbing).

undercanvas.com
24342 Presidio Ranch Road
+1 605 789 5194

LA PAUSE
Agafay Desert, Morocco

This desert camp is a one-hour drive south of Marrakech in the Agafay hills and a world away from the crowded souk. Guests stay in mud huts scattered around the property or in impromptu tents arranged according to guest configurations. The staff build what they need to for events (like weddings), then dismantle them to the dust. Days are spent exploring the area on mountain bikes or camels, or cooling off in the pool. Dinner is served under the stars. After sunset, candles are the only source of light.

lapause-marrakech.com
Douar Lmih Laroussiene
+212 06 10 77 22 40

CAMP WANDAWEGA
Elkhorn, Wisconsin, U.S.A.

A storied past (mobsters, speakeasies, prostitutes, and, somewhat anticlimactically, Latvian resort-goers) gives this idyllic Midwest haunt its character; the charm comes from its current owners, two creative directors with a hankering for flea markets, firewood, and plaid. Try your hand at the rope swing, dig out a canoe from the shed and glide across the calm water, join a game of tennis (the rackets come straight from the '20s, too), archery, or volleyball, or borrow one of the bikes and gallivant through the property and beyond.

wandawega.com
W5453 Lake View

Opposite page: Under Canvas
Mount Rushmore; this page,
top: La Pause; this page,
bottom: colorful suitcases at
Camp Wandawega

LIFE-CHANGING TIP #12

Gift Shops Worth Traveling For

Instead of basic toiletries and tourist tee-shirts, the best hotel boutiques sell local designer goods, artisanal food products, and luxury apothecary items. Don't fret if you've forgotten your toothbrush – you'll want to hit these gift shops anyway.

Poketo at The Line Hotel

São Lourenço do Barrocal Farm Shop

Beldi Country Club Shops

Poketo at The Line Hotel

Los Angeles, California, U.S.A.
A small outpost of the Los Angeles design shop sits adjacent to the lobby of Koreatown's hippest hotel and is filled with pharmacy basics, apparel designed exclusively for the property, and a stellar collection of stationery.
poketo.com
3515 Wilshire Boulevard
+1 213 381 7411

Ham Yard Village

London, England
Outside Ham Yard Hotel in London is a tree-filled pedestrian thoroughfare with 14 retail options, including a Brazilian swimwear boutique, an LA-inspired juice bar, a tea shop, a salon, and a theater.
firmdalehotels.com
One Ham Yard
+44 0 20 3642 2000

São Lourenço do Barrocal Farm Shop

Monsaraz, Portugal
This Alentejo farming village–turned–luxury farm retreat sits on nearly 2000 acres (8 square kilometers) of olive groves, vineyards, Neolithic ruins, and farmland – and has the sweetest little farm shop we ever did see. A curated mix of Portuguese goods are for sale, many of which can be seen around the hotel, including the Burel Factory wool blankets strewn at the end of each bed, blackwood picnic baskets used for lunch excursions, glazed earthenware from the restaurant, and chic bottles of estate-made olive oil.
barrocal.pt
7200-177 Monsaraz
+351 266 247 140

Beldi Country Club Shops

Marrakech, Morocco
The dense souks of Marrakech may sell more trinkets than any suitcase could ever hold, but a quick taxi from the center of town leads to the Beldi Country Club, an oasis in the city. Once past the hotel, gardens, pool, and restaurants, visitors find a series of boutiques and workshops making and selling textiles, glassware, ceramics, fashion items, and antiques. Everything is produced locally (in some cases on site), with a refined aesthetic, resulting in pieces that are much more interesting than the same-sameness typically found throughout the souk.
beldicountryclub.com
Km 6, Route de Barrage
+ 212 5 24 38 39 50, + 212 6 79 89 26 07

Freda

CLASKA Gallery & Shop "DO"

Drake General Store

Freda
New Orleans, Louisiana, U.S.A.
The tiny Marfa, Texas, shop has taken up residence at Ace Hotel New Orleans. Collaborating with makers from across the south, the lifestyle boutique has everything from handcrafted jewelry and clothing to beauty and gift items from local brands like Sara Ruffin Costello Clothing and Earth Reverie Jewelry.
acehotel.com
600 Carondelet St #130
+1 504 309 7515

Droog Shop Amsterdam
Amsterdam, The Netherlands
The single-room Hôtel Droog is part of a the Droog design complex — one building that offers shopping, dining, lectures, events, and a respite from it all on the top floor. The shop collection features prominent Dutch designers like Antoine Peters and Spijkers en Spijkers, small design products, Droog-label goods, and hard-to-find international beauty brands. Take a yoga class in the courtyard or visit the enchanting Fairy Tale Garden for a cup of tea.
droog.com
Staalstraat 7A/B
+31 0 20 523 50 50
9am–7pm

CLASKA Gallery & Shop "DO"
Tokyo, Japan
Tokyo's coolest boutique hotel is home to one of the country's best mini-lifestyle chains. The design shop has 13 outposts around Japan, each offering a selection of traditional crafts, ceramics, stationery, clothing, and beauty products from emerging Asian brands.
claska.com
1-3-18 Chuo-cho Meguro-ku
+81 3 3719 8124
11am–7pm

Farm Shop
Franschhoek, South Africa
While visiting Babylonstoren, a 17th-century Cape Dutch farm and inn an hour east of Cape Town, hotel guests can pick up a wide selection of items made from produce grown in the 8.5-acre (3-hectare) garden. Jams, cordials, preserves, soaps, and olive oil all make lovely souvenirs, as do a few bottles of wine from the hotel vineyard.
babylonstoren.com
+27 0 21 863 3852
9am–5pm

Drake General Store
Toronto, Canada
A cornucopia of our favorite shops all mixed into one, the Toronto flagship, located across the street from The Drake Hotel, combines the best of a classic general store, flea market, hotel gift store, and museum shop. Merchandise designed in-house is sold alongside limited-edition collabs and a roster of international and local brands. A mini cafe and rotating pop-ups are two extra touches exclusive to this location.
drakegeneralstore.ca
1151 Queen Street West
+1 416 538 2222
Monday–Saturday 10am–8pm, Sunday 11am–6pm

La Boutique by Les Bains Paris
Paris, France
The well-designed, art-filled Les Bains, former home of the legendary (and notorious) Paris nightclub of the same name, has a standalone concept shop and perfumerie located across the road. Artwork, skincare products and wooden skateboards are positioned alongside collaborations with luxury brands like Pierre Hardy and Delphine Delafon.
laboutique.lesbains-paris.com
+33 1 40 29 10 10

PART IX

Making It Last

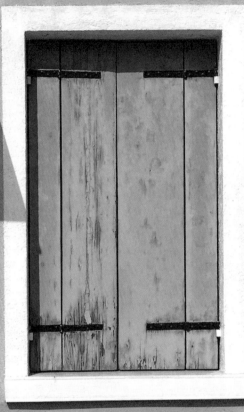

Let the Mind
Wander

Are we there yet?

We nearly are.

By now, you may have made a note or two about a city you want to visit or meal you want to try. Maybe you've resolved to go off-grid. Or just go somewhere – anywhere! – period. You understand that travel is about so many things – escape and joy, love and fear, effort and reward.

Glad to know we are on the same page.

Tourists have a fine time on holiday, but travelers are eyewitnesses ready for change – the mind-expanding, perception-modifying, occasionally (hopefully) life-altering kind of change. Of course, that kind of transformation is a lot to ask for when you're simply visiting friends in Los Angeles for the weekend or going to a family reunion in Adelaide.

But we can feel that change is afoot whenever we find ourselves looking at the familiar in a new light. When we imagine home in a new way when we're away from it. When we throw ourselves into uncomfortable situations and get out of them okay. When we live in the moment. There's even a stylish name for it: mindfulness.

Being mindful is not easy, especially when so much of the day-to-day feels like both a slog and a blur. Wake, work, eat, sleep, repeat. But travel offers an opportunity to break that pattern. By following three guidelines – anticipating the trip, slowing down while you're there, and riding the high once you're back – just about any travel experience can become more meaningful.

Opposite page: Colorful memories; this page: life's simple pleasures

ANTICIPATE

We all feel happier when we consciously delay our pleasure – booking that trip to Bora Bora six months in advance, for example, instead of buying a last-minute ticket – because it gives us time to think about how amazing everything will be.

If you're the kind of person prone to daydreaming, mood-boarding, and planning the details of every trip you take in meticulous shared Google spreadsheets, you're ahead of the game. Time and again, studies show that anticipating vacation can deliver pleasure in doses equal to or greater than actually being on vacation (even the kind that involves laying on a beach, frosty beverage in hand).

We have tried it both ways and we can feel the difference. This is why we are always in favor of total pre-trip immersion: read the books set in the destination, make the playlist of local bands, buy the swimsuit, watch the TV program, talk to friends, plot the routes, do a countdown (T-minus ten days to paradise!). Know that you can turn up the volume on happiness by actively savoring the future.

Opposite page: Bowls and olives from Greece; this page, top: it's spritz o'clock somewhere; this page, bottom: low-fi travel games

SLOW DOWN

Slow Travel is a deliberate attempt to eschew a checklist of "must-see" sights (Leaning Tower of Pisa! Spanish Steps! Pompeii! In seven days!) for real-deal experiences. The gist is to spend more time doing fewer things and doing them better.

That's not to say that you should abandon doing anything touristy at all; some things are popular for a reason. Obviously, when in Florence, you will visit the statue of David. It's one of the world's greatest sculptural marvels. But when you see it, take your time. Walk around. Sit down. Lay on the floor. Sketch a picture. Have a conversation with a fellow museum-goer or a guide. Be receptive, unhurried, reflective. Those qualities will allow you to truly enjoy what your vacation promised – the chance to feel relaxed and rejuvenated.

Instead of cramming, learn to savor. Tell yourself you have all the time in the world to be where you are. Imagine that you can come back in a few years if you want to. (Guess what? You can.) Linger over a lunch like you would if you lived around the corner. If you do a few things with meaning instead of a dozen that feel flimsy, you'll leave with a deeper appreciation and understanding of the places you've been. Don't do it all. Do it well.

RIDE THE HIGH

This part is so easily overlooked. Once you get back from your trip, you need a way to ride that glorious travel high.

As people who are particularly preoccupied with getting out of the house, we have to say that no matter where we go or how long we are gone, we are always delighted to come back home. It's true: we're a bunch of obsessive travelers who are also enthusiastic home cooks and happy couch potatoes. It's great to go away! It's great to be home! There's nothing odd or contradictory about this, either. Why can't you love both? You simply strive to make the most of your surroundings and your time, wherever you are.

But it's not just our nature – our jobs force us to be serial trip rehashers, too. Commiserating, researching, and reliving is what riding the high is all about.

Heading out into the great, wide world helps us appreciate our commonalities and our differences. If we give ourselves the chance to recount our experiences (on paper, online, in person), we have a better chance of adjusting our perspective and making lasting connections. It's a delicate balancing act – staying inspired while getting back into the swing of things – but taking the time to reminisce does the mind and body good.

LIFE-CHANGING TIP #13

Glorify the Experience

You came, you saw, you conquered. Now what can you do to make the most of your travels?

Throw a dinner party centered around the last place you visited. Go all out with the theme – tablescapes, recipes, music, after-dinner games, and storytelling.

Reframe your travel ephemera as artwork. Train tickets, brochures, and postcards can be matted and hung on the wall, an everyday reminder of a great vacation. Two online services that look super pro: Simply Framed (simplyframed.com) and Artifact Uprising (artifactuprising.com).

Go deep when the subject matter strikes a nerve: source the Croatian wine you fell for in Rovinj, watch the films of Studio Ghibli post–Mitaka tour, knit a sweater using the Alpaca wool you bought in Bolivia.

Adopt a new ritual for your everyday routine. Wear German house slippers around your apartment. Swap your robe for a yukata. Pour all your cider like an Asturian, which is to say, from 4 feet (1 meter) above the table into a glass – without looking.

Keep traveling at home. Watch movies filmed in locations where you've been. Read novels by local authors. Master a complicated paella, pho, or biryani. Burn a candle scented with cinnamon (Sri Lanka), lavender (Provence), or rose (Morocco).

Share your trinkets. Meet with friends to hand out souvenirs and pass along guidebooks – so that you can help them plan and anticipate the trip, and receive an extra dose of happiness along the way.

PART X

To Go

Essential Travel Tips and Hacks

You don't need to be a Million Miler to travel like a pro. A little bit of knowledge, organization, ingenuity, and small change goes a long way.

Keep your passport updated.
Check with the country that issued yours for more details. As a general rule, U.S. passports need to show at least six months of validity for international travel. If yours is set to expire before six months, renew it before you leave the country.

Keep travel essentials in one place at home.
If you keep the things you always need for a trip (like foreign currency, immunization records, travel blankets, and electrical adapters) in one drawer, you'll never have that 'Where's my passport?!' pre-flight panic again.

Invest in a good suitcase.
Preferably something with spinner wheels. You want to glide, not lug, your stuff.

Find out country requirements for entry.
Visit your state department or government's website to make sure your visas and vaccines are up to date.

Get the a-okay from your doctor.
Search by destination to see which vaccinations are recommended. This handy site caters to U.S. travelers, or a call to your primary care physician should do the trick. wwwnc.cdc.gov/travel/destinations/list

Be easy to find.
Look into the U.S. Department of State's Smart Traveler Enrollment Program (STEP) or your country's equivalent so your embassy or nearest consulate can contact you in an emergency.

Plan ahead to skip the lines.
For domestic travel within the U.S., enroll in TSA Pre-Check to make going through security quick and painless. If you travel internationally with regularity, enroll in Global Entry to sail through U.S. Customs. Even better, download the Mobile Passport app and skip the kiosk line, too.

Check your data plan before leaving.
Many cell phone companies offer options for staying connected while traveling abroad. Give them a call to find out your options.

Know your auto insurance.
Be clear about the insurance your credit card covers before you get to the rental counter.

Crowd-source travel advice.
Ask your network – friends, family, Instagram, Facebook – for tips on destinations.

Map in advance.
On Google Maps, star all the places you want to visit on your trip. Download the map on your phone for easy, offline access.

Read a novel set in the destination you're visiting.
Immerse yourself in a book about a place while you're there to get a whole new understanding of a foreign culture.

Update your app arsenal.
Think: meditation, workout, map, weather, currency converter.

Opposite page: Big Sur's rugged beauty

Get your emergency contacts in order.
Before a trip, make hard copies of your passport, itinerary, prescriptions, and important phone numbers. Keep a set at home and take a set with you. Make digital copies of the same documents: email a set to your parents/BFF/boss and upload them to the cloud.

Make the most of your credit card.
Get a no-fee version for international charges or an airline-specific card to earn points.

Invest in a reusable water bottle.
There's enough plastic in the ocean.

Stay charged.
Invest in a portable battery for your mobile phone. And carry it all the time, because phones have a way of dying at the worst possible moment.

Get electronics for two.
You'll be everyone's best friend at the lone outlet if you carry an outlet expander. And you and your pal can enjoy the same movie if you have a headphone splitter.

Make your luggage stand out.
Put a tag and/or ribbon on your suitcase to easily identify yours in a sea of black suitcases.

Travel with a deck of cards.
Leave it inside your suitcase so you don't have to remember to pack it.

Pack light.
Plan the clothes you want to take, then only pack half of that. You won't wear it all anyway.

Pack a go kit.
What would make your flight or ride more comfortable? Think headphones, ibuprofen, tissues, lip balm, eye drops, a pen, tea bags, gum, hand sanitizer, lotion – and put it all in a small bag for easy access.

Organize with small bags.
Pack your things in pouches – shoes, dirty laundry, wet bathing suits, electronics, underwear and socks – to keep things tidy and easily accessible. Bring an extra tote or zippered bag for souvenirs and in case your suitcase is overcrowded.

Pack breakables in the center of your suitcase.
Seal wine bottles in ziplock plastic bags before burying them among your socks and sweaters.

Pack the dopp kit once.
Keep your flight-friendly bag of 3-oz (100-ml) toiletries (toothbrush, toothpaste, shampoo, face wash, deodorant) packed at all times, and you won't have to pack it twice. If you vary your arsenal, keep a master checklist of the products you like to travel with, and you'll never forget anything.

Pack a scarf.
It does double duty as a blanket, sun shield, windbreaker, and takes up barely any space.

Pack a first aid kit.
Bandages for cuts and blisters, melatonin for crossing time zones, antacid for heartburn.

Bring extra meds.
If you take prescription drugs, bring more than you need in case your trip is delayed. And always carry them in your hand luggage.

Download your entertainment.
Load shows, songs, and books on your iPad or other devices the day before you travel.

Write things down on paper.
In case your phone battery betrays you: jot down the address and phone number of the place where you are staying.

Divide your cash and cards and pack a dummy wallet.

Keep your money, credit cards, and other important items split between bags and pockets. If you're traveling to a risky destination, carry a fake-out wallet (with a few bills and old cards) that will be easy to give up should a dangerous situation arise.

Avoid lost luggage panic.

Stash an extra set of underwear, socks, and toiletries, along with a small wad of cash, in your carry-on in case your checked baggage gets lost.

Look nice when you travel.

Wear something comfortable but not schleppy to the airport. Shoes that are easy to slip on and off, a few layers and accessories. You do not want to spend ten minutes undressing/dressing at security, and you want to look nice enough to be upgraded.

Get in the time zone.

As soon as you get on the plane, set your watch to local time at your destination.

Catch shut-eye on the plane.

For the closest thing to a good night's sleep, wear ear plugs and an eye mask. And a neck pillow will save your life on long-haul flights – the Trtl (trtltravel.com) is effective and small. Muji (muji. us) makes a handsome one in a more traditional shape and size.

Stretch on the airplane.

Get up and loosen up. When it's time to disembark, limber joints will help you hit the ground running.

Keep your phone tracker on.

For when you lose it.

Have a Plan B with your travel companions.

Talk about scenarios for dealing with emergencies and disasters and determine meeting places and backup plans ahead of time.

Carry small change for tips.

And break big bills as soon as you can.

Walk. Then walk some more.

The best way to get to know a new city is by walking through it. See something interesting? Pop your head in, say hello, and start a conversation.

Utilize public spaces.

If you want to use a clean bathroom or rest your feet, hotel lobbies can be welcoming and anonymous places. In case of an emergency, front desks are most likely to have English-speaking staff that's well informed. Public libraries are a nice place to take a quick snooze, use free internet, or source information.

Wear good walking shoes.

Vacation is not the time to break in a new pair of shoes.

Save your battery.

Set your phone to 'low power mode' even if you have 100 per cent battery to make it last longer.

Take pictures. Then put down the camera.

Photos are fun. But some of the best memories are made hands-free.

Make friends wherever you go.

Then you'll always have people to visit, couches to sleep on, dinner tables to sit at, postcards to send, and stories to tell.

Our Favorite Travel Products

Aesop Resurrection rinse-free soap cleanses and refreshes without water (aesop.com).

Anker PowerCore 10000 external battery charges devices at high speeds in a compact space (anker.com).

Apple AirPods make you feel free as a bird (apple.com).

Arlo Skye luggage has an unbreakable shell and built-in charger (arloskye.com).

Bach Rescue Remedy acts like a natural chill pill (bachflower.com).

Baggu reusable bags offer an extra set of hands just when you need them (baggu.com).

Bananagrams, let you spell words for fun and make time fly (bananagrams.com).

Cuyana leather travel case set encases your odds and ends in handcrafted leather (cuyana.com).

dōTerra OnGuard Beadlet: Protective Blend promotes immunity and freshens breath (doterra.com).

Dubs noise-cancelling ear plugs reduce volume without sacrificing sound (getdubs.com).

Flight 001 5-in-1 universal travel adapter powers devices in over 150 countries (flight001.com).

Flint lint roller retracts, refills, and smooths as it goes (meetflint.com).

Leatherology passport cover makes even the travel novice look pro (leatherology.com).

Lucas Papaw Ointment relieves burns, cuts, splinters, and rashes (lucaspapaw.com.au).

Native Union belt cable is long enough to reach badly placed airport outlets and durable enough to withstand non-stop travel. Plus, it's handsome (nativeunion.com).

Olio E Osso lip balm tints and hydrates all skin types (olioeosso.com).

Paravel packing cubes make the most of valuable suitcase real estate (tourparavel.com).

PurSteam travel steamer takes garments from crumpled to composed in 90 seconds (pursteam.us).

Rimowa luggage glides like a dream — thank you, German engineering (rimowa.com).

Trtl travel pillow casually holds up snoozing heads (trtltravel.com).

VinniBag inflatable travel bag provides a cozy air cushion for your favorite fragile souvenirs (ellessco.com).

Packing Lists

DOCUMENTS
And remember to have this all backed up online:
- ☐ passport
- ☐ visas
- ☐ license
- ☐ tickets/itinerary

GO-BAG
Keep this one handy for the flight:
- ☐ tissues
- ☐ pen
- ☐ moisturizer/lip balm
- ☐ ibuprofen
- ☐ hand sanitizer/wet wipes
- ☐ eye drops
- ☐ headphones
- ☐ deck of cards

TECH GEAR
- ☐ chargers (phone, laptop, tablet)
- ☐ converter
- ☐ extra battery (phone, camera)
- ☐ extra storage discs for camera

DOPP KIT
- ☐ shampoo/conditioner
- ☐ face wash
- ☐ moisturizer
- ☐ SPF
- ☐ soap/cleanser (preferably a gentle liquid that can double as laundry detergent)
- ☐ deodorant
- ☐ toothpaste/toothbrush/floss
- ☐ comb/hairbrush
- ☐ razor/shaving cream
- ☐ cotton pads/swabs
- ☐ nail file
- ☐ first-aid kit
- ☐ medications
- ☐ tampons
- ☐ condoms
- ☐ insect repellent

CLOTHES
- ☐ tee-shirts
- ☐ undergarments
- ☐ socks
- ☐ pants/jeans
- ☐ shirts
- ☐ dresses/skirts
- ☐ sweater
- ☐ jacket/blazer
- ☐ scarves/belts
- ☐ accessories/jewelry
- ☐ sneakers/dress shoes
- ☐ pjs
- ☐ swimsuit

AND DON'T FORGET
- ☐ games
- ☐ books
- ☐ corkscrew/bottle opener
- ☐ stationery

Index

About the Authors

JERALYN GERBA

Part pragmatist, part nostalgist, and wholehearted enthusiast of the irreverent, Jeralyn grew up in a house filled with books – history, fiction, science, reference – that stoked her curiosity for people, places, and things. She started traveling when she finally made enough money from summer jobs to do so, and, while based in New York City for university, she also studied art history in Italy, politics and society in South Africa, and food culture in Louisiana, among other things. She started writing about art, culture, nightlife, food, and items people make by hand, and figured out that she was happiest when comparing and collecting those observations with others.

She was hooked on visiting cities until she started hiking volcanoes, swimming in lagoons, and bicycle riding through rustic, unpaved lands. These days, her favorite destinations are places on the verge of change – probably because they are a visceral reminder that nothing is static, provide an opportunity to capture transformation in the making, and force her to embrace the unknown. For Jeralyn, travel feels the best when a challenge is met with a breakthrough and a homemade snack on the other side.

PAVIA ROSATI

Pavia boarded her first plane at nine months when her Italian mother took her to meet her grandparents at their villa outside Venice, a trip she repeated every year until college. As a result, her American classmates thought she was too Italian ("Where did you get those shoes?") and her Italian aunts thought she was too American ("You're eating *what* for dinner?"). Other early, formative trips saw her in pre-Perestroika Russia, where she learned to travel light, and post-Berlin-Wall Prague, where she learned to travel without a guidebook.

A voracious and tireless explorer who has lived in Paris, London and New York City, she has spent her career covering emerging talent in culture, entertainment, food, and travel. She is especially drawn to old homes and kitchens, because how we live the day-to-day speaks volumes about who we are and where we came from. She's at her best and happiest sitting around a table in animated conversation with new and old friends.

So far, Jeralyn and Pavia have visited 3 continents together and 6 separately. They have countless more journeys to log.

Acknowledgments

This book is a compilation of years of intel we have gathered from good trips, bad trips, press trips, honeymoons, family reunions, study abroads, library books, magazine stacks, as well as the invaluable intel we've received from our wonderful network of Fathom friends and contributors around the world. It would be impossible to make a book like this without the insights and input from our community.

Travel Anywhere would not have been possible without the invaluable contributions of Berit Baugher and Daniel Schwartz.

Senior editor Berit Baugher, Fathom's employee number one, has been with us through thick and thin, whether at a dining room table, an office cubicle, or a hotel lobby (of which there have been too many to count). Always the first to spot a new idea or trend, her discerning taste and appreciation for detail elevate every project we undertake.

Editor Daniel Schwartz, our man on the ground, is an even keel in the sometimes wild world of small business startups. Game for traveling anywhere, anytime, and tasting, testing, and photographing everything along the way, he is the best kind of traveler: energized and open to discovery.

A few people have been supporting our business since before we launched. We're looking at you, John D'Aquila, Juliana Jaoudi, Kenneth McVay, Bob Pittman, and Eliot Wadsworth. We'd also like to thank Primary, the co-working space we call home in NYC.

Stephanie March is our dear friend *and* our fairy godmother. One of the most inspiring travelers we know, we not only admire her sense of adventure but also her commitment to humanitarian advocacy.

Our family members are our favorite travel companions. Their support and encouragement have literally gotten us around the world and back. We may be writers, but words fail to convey the love and gratitude we feel for Justin and Gemma Carter, the Gerbas, Ben Schott, and Giacomo Rosati.

We'd also like to thank our Fathom team, contributors, and friends:

Abigail Radnor, Alpana Deshmukh, Alex Burgel, Anna Petrow, Becky Cheang, Camillia BenBassat and Team Avec, Christina Ohly, Crystal Meers, Delfina Forstmann, Erica Firpo, Helena Madrid, Jessica Cantlin, Kate Donnelly, Katie McKnoulty, Kelsey Burrow, Kim VanderVoort, Larkin Clark, Linda Cabasin, Matthew Pelc, Paul Jebara, Rachel Kurlander, Tess Falotico, and Victoria Lewis.

Like so many entrepreneurs who have more ideas than time, we have been wanting to write a book forever, but an inquiring over-the-transom email from Melissa Kayser was the spark that led to the book you're holding. Thank you to the Hardie Grant team — Jane Grant, Megan Cuthbert, Allison Hiew, and Renee Senogles — for making the process of producing a book across continents a seamless and wonderful collaboration. We are already jotting down notes for the second edition.

A most special and final thanks to you, dear reader, for spending time with us in the world. We began Fathom to share our discoveries, and that would be meaningless without someone to share them with. We'd love to know where you are going also, so please tag your adventures #TravelwithFathom on Instagram and say hi to us on all the socials at @FathomWaytoGo.

Top: Team Fathom: Daniel, Pavia, Jeralyn, Berit; bottom: authors Jeralyn Gerba and Pavia Rosati

PHOTO CREDITS

Images courtesy of the following photographers and businesses: (Letters indicate where multiple images appear on a page, from top to bottom, left to right)

Phaisal Photos/Unsplash front cover; Tom Grimbert/Unsplash back cover a; Ricardo Gomez/Unsplash back cover c; Austin Motel back cover c; Alpana Deshmukh ii, 168, 169, 170a, 170b; The Traveling Light 2; Daniel Schwartz 4a, 20b, 171, 185a, 185b; Pavia Rosati 4b, 19a, 21, 94a, 94b, 158b, 159, 163a; Larkin Clark 4c, 9a, 13a, 16b, 16c; Justin Carter 5; Fynn Schmidt/Unsplash 8; Nicola Brasetti/Unsplash 9b; Rolf Gelpke/Unsplash 10-11; Jessica Cantlin 12; Sylvain Cleymans/Unsplash 13b; Martin Widenka/Unsplash 13c; Berit Baugher 14, 79b, 112a, 174; Mark Gray 15; Ross Belfer 16a; Tom Grimbert/ Unsplash 18; Pablo García Saldaña/Unsplash 19b; Mike Yukhtenko/Unsplash 20a; Jorge Tung/Unsplash 22-23; Christopher Czermak/Unsplash 24a; Jack Anstey/Unsplash 24b; Harshil Gudka/Unsplash 24c; Ryo Yoshitake/Unsplash 25; Dave Shaw/Unsplash 26-27; Rory Doyle 30, 35a, 35b, 35c; Courtesy of Bahia Bustamante 31; Courtesy of Linkum Tours 32; Courtesy of Eremito 33; Chris Burkard 34a, 34b; Anthony Grote 36; Courtesy of Sal Salis Ningaloo Reef 38-39; Courtesy of Wild Bush Luxury 40-41; Moritz Krebs / courtesy of Soneva Fushi 42; Courtesy of Intrepid Travel 43, 46-47; Courtesy of The Ranch Malibu 44, 45b; Ji Pak/Unsplash 45a; Courtesy of Natural Selection 48a; Courtesy of Whynot Adventure 48b, 48c; Ralph Lee Hopkins / courtesy of Natural Habitat Adventures 49; Courtesy of Coral Expeditions 50, 51a; Courtesy of Robin Pope Safaris 51b; Amy Murrell 54, 56b; Eric Wolfinger 55a; Sharon Cairns / courtesy of Jackalope 55b, 57; Garrett Rowland 56a; Erik Olsson / courtesy of Faviken 59; Courtesy of Babylonstoren 60-61; Melanie Lewis of The Mhor Collection 62a, 62b, 62c, 62d; Courtesy of Belmond Le Manoir aux Quat'Saisons 63; Courtesy of Serenbe 64; J. Ashley 65a; Ali Harper 65b; Courtesy of Don Alfonso 1890 66; Magnus Mårding 67a, 67c; Claudio Aversa 67b; beall + thomas photography 68a, 68b; Charity Burggraaf 68c, 70-71; Nicolas Castillo / courtesy of Vik Retreats 69; Galen Crout 72; Courtesy of La Grenouillère 73a, 73b; Marion Michele/Unsplash 76; Max van den Oetelaar/Unsplash 77; Zhgn_/Unsplash 78; Taylor Davis/Unsplash 79a; Yulinar Rusman/Unsplash 81a; Paolo Bendandi/Unsplash 81b; Kalle Kortelainen/Unsplash 82-83; Madalena Veloso/ Unsplash 84; Robert Bye/Unsplash 85a; Jeralyn Gerba 85b, 112b, 113a, 132c, 149a, 153b; Andrew Charney/Unsplash 86-87; Courtesy of Hubud 90; Matt Garies/Unsplash 92-93; Courtesy of Telliskivi Creative City 95a, 95b; Jared Rice/Unsplash 96-97; Judah Guttmann/Unsplash 98; Néstor Morales/Unsplash 99; Courtesy of The Working Capitol 100; Franz Navarette / courtesy of Hubud 101a ; Courtesy of Ministry of New 101b; Courtesy of Crew Collective 102; Courtesy of ninetytwo13 by Tokyo Chapter 103a; Annie Spratt/Unsplash 103b; courtesy of Hubud 104-105; Jason Cooper/Unsplash 110; Gabriel Jimenez/Unsplash 111; Midhun George/Unsplash 113b; Lava Lavanda/Unsplash 113c; Marc Lecureuil 114; Owen Morgan / courtesy of The Great Projects 115; Abigail Keenan/ Unsplash 116-117; Daniel Burka/Unsplash 118-119; Pia Riverola 122; Alex Fradkin 124, 125a, 125b; Courtesy of Shipwreck Lodge/Natural Selection 126a; Courtesy of Aman 126b; César Béjar 127; Courtesy of Casa Bonay 128, 144; Charles Reagan 129; Y. Deguchi 130-131; Tim Wright/Unsplash 132a; Undine Pröhl 132b; Chris Spira 132d, 133; Adrian Gaut 134; Courtesy of Ett Hem 135a, 135b; Courtesy of Zero George 136; Kara Rosenlund 137a; Nick Simonite 137b, 138c, 143a, 143b, 146-147, 148a; Courtesy of Wythe Hotel 138a; Courtesy of American Trade Hotel 138b; Simon Brown 139; Courtesy of Zannier Hotels 140, 142; Courtesy of Alila Hotels & Resorts 141a; Courtesy Liberty Hotel 141b; Elsa Hahne 145a; Courtesy of Sir Savigny Hotel 145b; Courtesy of Alabama Hotel 148b; Pedro Silva Correia149b; Courtesy of Tribal Hotel 150-151; Courtesy of Island Outpost 152, 154c, 155; Thomas Habr/Unsplash 153a; Courtesy of L'Hotel 154a; Courtesy of The Savoy Hotel 154b; Courtesy of Villa Feltrinelli 156, 157a; George Apostolidis 157b; Courtesy of Delaire Graff Lodges and Spa 158a; Grégoire Gardette / courtesy of La Réserve Paris 158c; Courtesy of Jesse Walsh + Dreamtown Co. 160, 162; Courtesy of Ventana Big Sur, an Alila Resort 161a; Courtesy of Wild Coast Tented Lodge 161b; Chris Strong 163b; Courtesy of Poketo at The Line Hotel 164a; Ash James 164b ; Courtesy of Beldi Country Club 164c; Alex Marks 165a; Courtesy of CLASKA Gallery & Shop "DO" 165b; Courtesy of Drake General Store 165c

Published in 2019 by Hardie Grant Travel, a division of
Hardie Grant Publishing

Hardie Grant Travel (Melbourne)
Building 1, 658 Church Street
Richmond, Victoria 3121

Hardie Grant Travel (Sydney)
Level 7, 45 Jones Street
Ultimo, NSW 2007

www.hardiegrant.com/au/travel

A catalogue record for this
book is available from the
National Library of Australia

Travel Anywhere (and Avoid Being a Tourist)
ISBN 9781741176544

10 9 8 7 6 5 4 3 2 1

Publisher
Melissa Kayser

Senior editor
Megan Cuthbert

Editor
Allison Hiew

Proofreader
Julie Yerex

Editorial assistance
Rosanna Dutson

Design
Lila Theodoros

Typesetting
Kerry Cooke

Index
Max McMaster

Prepress
Kerry Cooke and Splitting Image Colour Studio

Printed and bound in China by LEO Paper Group